ACT FOR HEALTH

Using Theater to Teach Tough Teen Topics

R. WILLIAM PIKE

ETR Associates
Santa Cruz, California
1991

ETR Associates (Education, Training and Research) is a nonprofit organization committed to fostering the health, well-being and cultural diversity of individuals, families, schools and communities. The publishing program of ETR Associates provides books and materials that seek to empower young people and adults with the skills to make positive health choices. We invite health professionals to learn more about our high-quality resources and our training and research programs by contacting us at P.O. Box 1830, Santa Cruz, CA 95061-1830.

Published by ETR Associates, P. O. Box 1830,
Santa Cruz, California 95061-1830.
Printed in the United States of America.
Designed by Julia Chiapella.
10 9 8 7 6 5 4 3 2
Title No. 595

Library of Congress Cataloging-in-Publication Data

Pike, R. William.
    Act for health : using theater to teach tough teen
topics / R. William Pike.
        p. cm.
    ISBN 1–56071–067-5
    1. Drama in education. 2. Theater and youth.
3. Theater—Production and direction. 4. Social
problems. I. Title.
PN3171.P53 1992
373.1'332—dc20   91-28476
                                                    CIP

For Ann and Chris.

Table of Contents

Preface

ta · boo´: 1. Among primitive tribes, a sacred prohibition put upon certain people, things, or acts which makes them untouchable or unmentionable. 2. A ban or inhibition attached to something by social custom or emotional aversion.
—*The American Heritage Dictionary*

As a teacher, I sometimes feel as though I am living and working "among primitive tribes." One would automatically assume that I am, of course, referring to the students I teach. In part, I am. A sophomore English class can turn savage when faced with the prospect of reading *Julius Caesar*. However, fellow teachers, administrators, members of the board of education and community members would also exhibit "primitive tendencies" if faced with the life-threatening problems which confront our young people every day.

Drug and alcohol abuse, suicide, teen pregnancy, sexual abuse, physical abuse and AIDS are all issues which touch many of the kids sitting in the classrooms of America. Unfortunately, many of these topics have become "taboo," that is, unmentionable. For any number of reasons, kids indeed feel an emotional aversion toward speaking about the abuse they experience, sharing their suicidal feelings with someone who could help, or telling a parent about a pregnancy. This reluctance to disclose short circuits any mechanisms in place which may help them through the crisis.

Several years ago, I chose to address this reluctance through theater. With the help of a social worker, my theater classes and I began to write scenes, monologues, poems and songs that encouraged kids in crisis to reach out for help, to form a bridge of communication between themselves and a friend, a parent, a teacher or a trained professional. Our feeling was that the best way to get through to kids was to have other kids present the message (kids teaching kids). This approach would augment standard curriculum in a *unique* way: a way that might spark attention, a way that the student might remember and a way that would encourage a student to *do something* about the crisis he or she was facing. These were our goals. We didn't know if we could achieve them. We didn't know if the process would work.

Our first production included scenes on suicide, sexual abuse, physical abuse and date rape. Several days later, a girl approached the social worker and made an appointment to talk about "that play" she had seen. The day before she made her appointment, she was beaten and raped by her boyfriend. The social worker could only guess why the girl had made the appointment, but she credited our performance with giving her the courage to come forward.

This story helped me decide to continue to try to break the chain of abuse, using the theater as a vehicle. This book outlines the vehicle, so that others can benefit from and use our experience.

Deciding to help a young person at risk and identifying the patterns of abuse are relatively easy tasks. Breaking the patterns is not. *Act for Health* strives to help break the patterns, to expose the situations and to reach teenagers who feel there is nothing worth reaching for.

There are many people who have contributed to this project over the years. Among those who should be acknowledged are Rosemary Fretto, Ellen Katims, Donna Gaspari, Edie Wagner, Alice Pike and the scores of young people who contributed their energy, creativity and compassion to help others.

Introduction

On April 8, 1990, Ryan White died of AIDS in an Indiana University hospital room. Before his death, he had emerged in the hearts and minds of the world as a symbol of the fight against AIDS, as the embodiment of humanism, as a force against ignorance, and as a reminder of the frailty of us all.

Ryan White was eighteen when he died. He lived much of his adolescence struggling with AIDS and striving to educate society about a new and frightening illness. His life and death serve to demonstrate the many complex problems young people face in today's society.

At Ryan's funeral, rock singer Elton John chose to honor him by singing an old song about Marilyn Monroe called "Candle in the Wind."

> *It seems to me you lived your life*
> *Like a candle in the wind*
> *Never knowing who to cling to*
> *When the rain set in... * *

---

* Written by Elton John and Bernie Taupin. Copyright ©1975 Dick James Music, Ltd. All rights for the United States and Canada controlled by Songs of PolyGram International, Inc.

In describing Ryan White's life as a "candle in the wind," John was describing the lives of many other young people today as well. Too many adolescents don't know "who to cling to"; too many don't know where to turn, or where to find help.

It is not surprising that Elton John chose to honor Ryan White in song. Music, poetry and drama have often been used to express emotion, to communicate feelings and to help ease the pain. In turn, it is not surprising that music, poetry and drama have emerged as powerful tools for confronting the many taboo issues that plague today's young adults.

Act for Health is essentially a learning tool that relies on writing and performance for its strength. You don't have to be a great writer to use it and you don't have to be a great actor to perform it. The book's focus is upon communication. As long as that communication is genuine and heart-felt, the process will be successful.

Throughout the book the words "teacher" and "student" are used. They are general labels which may be applied in various ways. The "teacher" may be a guidance counselor, a scout leader, a high school health teacher, a social worker, a community or church volunteer, a parent or a drama coach. "Teacher" is used to identify anyone who oversees the project, helps to organize ideas and keeps an objective control over what will grow into a very subjective experience. If a "teacher" cares about kids, he or she is amply qualified to use this book.

The label "student" may be applied to anyone. The "students" who would benefit from this program could range in age from twelve to seventy-five. However, the materials presented in this volume are *directly* aimed at "students" in their adolescence (grades seven through twelve).

The key element of *Act for Health* is that young people are teaching other young people. The teacher should be viewed as the engine of the project and the students as the engine's fuel. Students write the material, perform the material and view the material. However, even though the program is student-centered, the teacher must carefully provide guidance through each stage.

The quality of the relationship established between teacher and students is paramount. At every step, the teacher depends upon the students for their insight and creativity and the students depend upon the teacher for his or her objectivity and organizational skills. How much the teacher or the students are involved in each step of the program is totally dependent upon that relationship. Obviously, the better the relationship, the better the program.

This book is divided into three sections: *The Script, The Performance,* and *Sample Scripts.* Followed step-by-step, it is a total educational experience. It is a cycle of learning/teaching/learning accomplished by the students themselves.

The Script details a procedure a teacher may follow to create materials that address the problems of AIDS, drug and alcohol abuse, suicide, pregnancy, sexual abuse and physical abuse. In and of itself, the writing of a script is a valuable endeavor. Students work together to research topics, to discuss which issues and which messages need to be examined, and, finally, to construct the most effective and dramatic way to present them to an audience.

The Performance provides the steps necessary to present the scripts that have been written to an audience. It examines how to cast the scenes, discusses the ideas of good education vs. good performance, explains how to prepare both the audience and the participants for their experience and explores how to handle student disclosures.

Finally, *Sample Scripts* are provided for use by teenagers and demonstrate what can be achieved by following the program to its conclusion. All of these scripts were developed by students and teachers in a workshop setting and all have been presented with success to student audiences from grades eight through twelve. The scripts were designed to encourage discussion and foster disclosure. Teachers are encouraged to adapt the ideas presented here and to apply them to their own special situations.

Ultimately, how this book is used must be determined by the teacher, scout leader, peer counselor, or drama student who reads it. However, throughout the process, the participants should never lose sight of Ryan White, his struggle to live and his battle against ignorance.

The Script

The most essential point to remember when writing these scripts is *always* write for an audience. *Always* write as though your scene will be performed for an audience of hundreds. In this way, your scenes will be creative and alive instead of pedantic and static.

Even though you must always write for an audience, you actually have the option to perform the scenes or to simply go through the writing process. This decision must be made by the teacher before any writing begins. Talk with your students to determine their interest in performance and to decide if a performance is feasible in your particular school, church or community.

Once this decision has been made, stow it away and forget it. Proceed with the program as though performance were the ultimate objective. The preparations for the writing, the research, the discussion and the revision are all essential components of the educational process. None should be omitted simply because you may not be performing what has been written.

Should performance be your ultimate goal, you are free to explore limitless possibilities of expression. Monologues are wonderful if you have only a few students with which to work. Group oral presentations work very well if your students are either mostly female or mostly male. Full-blown scenes work well in any situation. Whenever possible, exploit the musical talents of your students and include original songs, lyrics and musical compositions.

Communication is the key. If you make the language true, the emotions sincere and the messages powerful, you will have created an unstoppable educational machine.

The Scope of the Project

Before you prepare your material for presentation, you will need to decide on the scope of your project.

One goal may be to perform this material simply for your class. Depending on time constraints, student and teacher experience, and abilities, you may want to avoid the added work and pressure of performing for "strangers." As a simple class project, you may want to write the scenes, then read them aloud in class. You could publish a class book of the plays, avoiding the idea of performance altogether. Keeping your work within your class is a valuable and worthy goal.

You will obviously reach the broadest audience when your class performs their material for other classes in various disciplines and on various grade levels. This goal is the most ambitious, creates the most work, causes the most headaches, and reaps the most rewards.

If you wish to perform your scripts, consider presenting your material to other classes in your discipline.

Possibly all health classes could work on scenes and present them to each other. Perhaps a biology class could join together with a family living class and share material.

There are many questions you must ask yourself should you decide to tread this path. Who will your audience be? Will they be elementary students? Will there be Special Education students in the audience?

It has been the experience of many high school guidance counselors and social workers that students often enter high school having already been victimized. The "window of victimization" is much greater during the elementary and junior high school years.

It is for this reason that many of the scripts for high school students focus on disclosure. Our messages encourage high school students to share what they have been going through.

On the elementary level, "no-go-tell" is the message. On the junior high level, recognition and prevention of the abusive act are the focus.

Unfortunately, abuse may occur at any time before, during, or after an adolescent enters high school. Therefore, recognition, prevention and disclosure are important messages for any age group. These categories are broad and are intended to make student writers think about which message is best for their audience.

In addition to a student audience, your group may perform for other teachers, administrators, school psychologists, members of the board of education or community members. Ask yourself why each of these audiences is there viewing the work. Teachers may want to see if they could adapt the process for their own classes. You may be asking the school psychologist to attend a performance to review the messages the scenes are sending and to weed out any inconsistencies or misinformation. Administrators, board members and parents will need to see the program to confirm that the content is appropriate for presentation to the students (censorship and appropriateness will be discussed in later sections).

A challenge to your students—and an important component of the project—is learning to focus the material to consider all the issues that affect your broad audience base. Scripts should never be altered for a specific audience (e.g., taking out profanity for an audience of parents and then reinserting it for a student audience). The time to alter a scene comes after you have feedback from your audience. Listen carefully to their reactions and adjust your material accordingly.

Choosing a Topic

The next step in creating materials for your class is to identify the problems to confront. Unfortunately, there are a host of issues to tackle. Narrow down all of the possibilities and focus upon only a few specific areas.

At this point, the relationship between teacher and student is tested. The teacher must encourage a wide range of suggestions from the students while at the same time working to narrow down the topics.

A good way to begin this narrowing-down process is to ask students to name topics that are important to their lives as well as to their school or community.

Never force a topic. Let the topics flow naturally from the concerns of the students and their community. You may feel personally that interracial dating is a pressing issue to explore. If your students don't, however, skip it. They know best.

Abuse, social pressure, self-esteem, smoking, racial tensions and divorce are all broad areas which can be effectively presented. Select one or two; too many issues will cloud your message and confuse both your students and your audience.

Another effective way to narrow the list of possible topics is to have students meet with administrators, social workers, guidance counselors and parents to assess the needs of the school and community. If teenage pregnancy is a school and community concern, and your students agree, focus on that topic and leave other issues to other projects.

As you get deeper and deeper into the process, you will discover that many topics are tied together. Very often, one contributing cause of physical abuse is a parent who is also abusing alcohol; so, if you are writing a scene on physical abuse, you may have to touch upon alcoholism. If you are addressing teen suicide, you will probably have to discuss self-esteem. Allowing for certain overlapping issues, try to keep your focus tight and your concentration on one major issue at a time.

It is essential that students have some sort of personal interest in their project topic. If they do, what they write and how they perform will be more believable. Usually, it is disastrous to divide up the class evenly and delegate topics arbitrarily.

One way to handle topic decisions is to have the class decide which issues they feel strongly about. Then prepare sign-up sheets for each issue and have students sign up for the topic of their choice. Stress that students sign up for a topic because of its interest to them, not because their friends are signing up for it.

Giving students control over the situation at the beginning gives them the authority over what they write. You will find that in addition to eagerly assuming authority, they will assume ownership of what they write and a sense of pride.

Before You Start to Write
Involving Administrators, Staff and Parents

Once the group is committed to specific topics, the teacher must begin to consider what effect exploring these topics will have on the school and community. How will administrators react to controversial issues? What will parents think about discussing sexual topics? How will your students deal with explicit sexual references? Finally, how will disclosures from student writers be handled?

Before these questions can be answered, the teacher must assess the district's views on controversial topics. Discuss the content of the proposed scenes with an administrator who "speaks for the school district." What will they support? What will they disapprove?

A district administrator can be a very valuable asset to you. He or she may know the community better than you do, and be able to predict reactions to your material. There may be explosive reactions from the administration or the community at the mere mention of AIDS, abortion or contraception. The more you know about how your community might react, the better you will be able to speak to them in each scene and to tailor each message so that it will strike home. Your administration will also know whether there are district guidelines for dealing with sensitive issues in the classroom. Making sure you are completely informed about controversial subjects that may come up will save wasted efforts in the long run.

It would be ideal if the students were involved in this part of the process. Their input and their ideas would enlighten administrators about sensitive issues. However, since the perspective of the students may differ from the perspective of the school district, and since both are valid, be prepared to act as a sideline referee.

Over the years, I have been fortunate to work closely with one specific social worker and one district administrator, both of whom deal with students in crisis. Without their continued advice and "professional eyes," my programs would not have been as comprehensive or successful.

It would be to your advantage to contact such people at a very early stage. Explain how they can be of help and ask to meet with them several times over the course of the project. If you have asked the right people, they will seize the opportunity, roll up their sleeves and jump into the project with you.

You will also need to think about parents and how to involve them. At the very least, you should encourage your students to discuss with their parents what they are doing in class. Offer to speak to any parent who may have questions or objections. In ten years, parents who've called me have shown nothing but support for our efforts. This is not to say that there won't ever be any opposition to what you are doing. Be prepared to defend your project, then be pleasantly surprised when you receive nothing but praise.

Your district may have a policy that states that parents must be notified if their child will be working with sensitive subjects. A letter home may be required and permission may be necessary. Be careful not to create a problem where one does not exist. In your letter, discuss the topics you will be working with; be positive about the program. Invite parents to talk with you should they have any questions or need more information.

Last year, several weeks prior to the first performance, our school held Parent's Night. I made it a point to discuss the content of the program with the parents of the students involved. I readied myself for confrontations. None came. I received nothing but support for the program as a whole, and for the specific messages we were conveying about controversial issues.

Legal Concerns

You must now become aware of state and local disclosure laws and how they might apply to the program. Teachers may be required, by law, to divulge any information a student writer reveals concerning past or ongoing abuse. Many tough legal and ethical questions arise here and you must know how to handle them.

Will you "turn in" a student who has confided in you? Are you prepared to lose your job in order to keep a student's confidence? Are you comfortable telling student writers to be open and genuine at all times, but also to be aware that you may have to report everything they say or write? Unfortunately, there are no easy answers to any of these questions.

The best people to touch base with over concerns such as these are school counselors, school psychologists or school social workers. These people can provide valuable legal information, important background on school and community trouble spots and be a good sounding board for any ethical questions you may have regarding student disclosures. (Don't be surprised if you begin to feel the need for a little counseling yourself. Someone to talk to who understands your project and its scope is a valuable commodity.)

Getting Comfortable with Sensitive Issues

Because you may face opposition and because the topics you are dealing with may be sensitive, it is essential that you and your class be thoroughly prepared.

Carefully discuss with the class what is expected of them and exactly what they will be doing. If you are going to be working with the issue of sexual abuse, for example, give the class plenty of time to get comfortable with the terms and ideas they will be writing about.

You may need to do some work in this area as well. Initially, it is very difficult to speak in sexually explicit language if you are not a health or biology teacher by trade. If you are uncomfortable with the language, the class and ultimately the audience will be uncomfortable with it as well. You and your class must get used to discussing intercourse, describing the scene of a suicide, or exploring what the victim of incest must feel. Without tackling these terms and ideas head-on, your material will be cold, sterile, impersonal and ineffective. If you want your audience to be moved, first you and your class must be moved.

Ironically, after spending several weeks on a project, there is a danger of becoming overly familiar with the issues. After being repeated over and over for two months, the line, "Mom, Uncle Bob raped me," begins to lose its impact. Partially because of overfamiliarity and partially because of stress, there is the potential to make light of the issues. Sometimes a release from the seriousness is healthy. However, maintaining respect for your material and its content is essential. Help students remember there may be members in the audience for whom the story may be intensely personal.

Learning About the Topic

Once you've chosen your topics you'll need to help students educate themselves about their issues. Much of the work you and your classes will produce will be fiction. Ideas will come from things the students have heard from friends, stories they have read, or from movies or TV. For student writers to accurately depict true-to-life issues in a fictional setting, they will need some footing in reality.

Invite a social worker, guidance counselor or school psychologist to talk to your students about the problems in their school or community. It is most effective if the speaker can give examples of actual case studies or personal stories about the topics you are addressing. The more personal the story, the more your class will be moved. The more your class is moved, the better they will write and the better they will perform.

After the lecture, review with your class the major

issues that were touched upon. Have them write down anything that affected them in any way: facts that surprised them, ideas that bothered them, statistics they didn't believe. These reactions are the kernels for the scenes and monologues to follow. They are the emotional core to be built upon.

In addition to using guest speakers as information sources, turn to your school and community libraries for additional material. There are a host of excellent research tools available which deal specifically with many sensitive subjects.

Two resources that provide valuable factual material on current social issues are *SIRS* and *PROQUEST.*

SIRS, The Social Issues Resource Series, published by SIRS, Inc., provides timely information in an easy-to-use, accessible format. The series includes 32 volumes of articles reprinted from various periodical sources. Its strength lies in the fact that each volume discusses a relevant social issue (Sexuality, Crime, Family, Medicine) and each volume has an extensive index and cross-reference guide.

PROQUEST is a state-of-the-art, computerized information retrieval system from University Microfilms International. *PROQUEST* Periodical Abstracts Ondisc provides abstracts and articles from over four hundred general interest, scientific and special interest journals.

Scenes Based on Personal Experience

Occasionally you may find that a student has written a gripping account of an abusive act, and you know deep down, that the scene is the truth, not fiction. You know the student is painstakingly describing what he or she has personally experienced.

You can confront this situation in a variety of ways. First, talk to the student privately and praise the work. Tell the student that the material really captured the true feeling of the topic. Then, ask how he or she could give such vivid descriptions. By this time, the student should realize what you are trying to get at. The student will either dismiss your implications or admit that the story is true.

If the student dismisses your fears as unfounded, there is nothing more you can do but keep a close eye on him or her. You may want to contact a social worker or guidance counselor at this point, and have them follow-up your suspicions.

If the student admits that the material was indeed fact, you have a serious situation. First, assess the student's feelings toward the writing. Is the issue something that happened years ago and has been properly taken care of? Is this an incident that happened recently and is still undisclosed? In either case, it is best to seek a professional's help.

If the student has never disclosed the abusive act, the situation becomes more complicated. The student may beg you not to tell anyone. Even though you want nothing more than to be accommodating, there is no way you can keep silent and try to help the student by yourself. Work with a social worker or guidance counselor to decide on the best approach to take with the student, but be sure that you, the teacher, follow up.

Several years ago, a student wrote a gripping monologue about a girl who hated her mother and was planning suicide. It jumped out at me and shouted "real." I praised the girl for her writing, but confronted her. She quickly admitted that the monologue was based on truth and begged me not to tell anyone about it, especially not her mother. She wanted her work used in the production, but she wanted to remain anonymous. I realized that even though she thoroughly believed she wanted me to do nothing about what she had written, the mere fact that she'd written it and submitted it to me was a cry for help. After a long talk, I finally convinced her that we should go to her guidance counselor.

We all met, the counselor thanked me for bringing the situation to his attention and told me that he would handle the problem from then on. Several weeks passed and the girl and I never spoke of the matter again. I noticed that she was a bit cool toward me, but I credited that to the pain she must be going through in confronting her feelings. I assumed she was working with the counselor and that all was progressing well.

I then had an opportunity to speak with the girl's mother. I praised her daughter's work and told her how valuable her daughter had been to the program. I also expressed my relief that her problems had finally come to the surface and were now getting proper attention. The mother looked at me and asked, "What problems?" Suddenly I realized that neither the daughter nor the counselor had spoken to the mother about the girl's suicidal feelings. I considered asking the woman to speak with the guidance counselor or with her daughter, but that would have magnified her fears. I told her the story; she was completely ignorant of her daughter's feelings or of the fact that anything could have possibly been wrong.

It took several weeks and several meetings to bring some order to the chaos that erupted. But that chaos was infinitely better than the daughter harboring destructive thoughts. The message of this episode is clear. We must tread carefully with both our material and our students because we are dealing with potentially explosive situations.

Handling Student Disclosures

Both you and your students must now begin to think about the disclosure of abuse. It is too early in the process for any outside audience disclosures. However, it is not too early for *your* students to disclose information regarding their personal experiences with abuse.

One year, before we began the project, I asked a group of about thirty students a few questions. Their answers both surprised and disturbed me.

"How many of you know someone who has been raped?"

About a half-dozen hands went up.

"How many of you know someone who has a parent with a substance abuse problem?"

Half the class raised their hands.

"How many of you know someone who has attempted suicide?"

Again, about half the class. Finally ...

"How many of you know a girl who became pregnant while either in junior high or high school?"

Almost every student raised a hand.

Not only do these answers reveal the magnitude of these problems, they also indicate that, most likely, you will have several students working on the program who are victims of abuse themselves.

If you have been careful, you will already have established an atmosphere of care and concern. Students may feel secure enough to share their experiences with you and with the other students. In one sense, it is almost easier for a teacher to make decisions regarding such disclosures. Teachers are often bound by law or school policy to follow certain procedures in a disclosure situation. Students find themselves in a unique and special position when they are the ones to whom a disclosure is made.

Understandably, many young people feel more comfortable telling a close friend or classmate (rather than an adult) about problems they are experiencing or about abuse that took place in the past. Depending upon the severity of the disclosure, students should listen carefully, show support and, ideally, advise the student who is disclosing to speak to an adult. The focus of handling a disclosure should be on helping the student find help, *not* on keeping the disclosure a secret from parents, teachers or guidance counselors.

Revealing disclosures to adults is an easy suggestion to make, but may be a very difficult task for some students to reconcile. Are you asking them to go against the wishes of a close friend who has just reached out to them? Are you asking them to "rat someone out"? No. You are asking them to guarantee that a friend gets the help that he or she desperately needs.

Even though friends or classmates can provide essential compassion and support, they may not be able to provide the resources needed to handle a serious problem. Support personnel, counselors, teachers and social workers know where to guide a student in crisis so that the problem can be taken care of immediately.

Even though adult support personnel may be the key to properly handling student disclosures, your students once again emerge as the strongest link between an adolescent in trouble and an adult who can help.

Stress to your students that by agreeing to keep a disclosure secret, they may be prolonging the abuse they are trying to stop. At the risk of sounding melodramatic, how your students handle student disclosures could very well be a matter of life or death.

Writing the Script

Once students have a clear picture of what they want to write, you have the blessings of the administration, and you and your students are comfortable with and knowledgeable about your topics, it is time to put pen to paper. The writing process may be divided into three stages: initial writing, group revision and individual revision. Get your students used to rewriting; it is the most important part of the process.

This is also a good time to start to prepare the class that not all scenes will be performed. It's tough to spend so much time and effort on material only to discover that it didn't shape-up well enough to be performed. Tell the class that certain scenes might be cut because there is a strict time limit. The class doesn't have an unlimited amount of time to revise the material. Because the revision process is done aloud and as a group usually, the students will probably know which scenes are working and which scenes are not. Often students may actually welcome the teacher's decision to cut a scene because it removes them from a situation that they knew wasn't succeeding. The most difficult aspect of cutting a scene is for the teacher to summon the courage to do it.

Initial Writing

Initial writing should take approximately one to two weeks. Don't plan to spend less than one week if you want to glean anything of substance. Give students time in class to throw ideas around and to read lines aloud to their group members. Suggest that each group select one student to go home each night and polish what the group accomplished in class.

At the initial writing stage, too many dissonant choices in a writing group sometimes impede progress. Several people may want to go in several different directions with the scene. Suggest that each begin separately and bring written ideas back to the group for discussion and compromise.

You will always encounter students who refuse to write with other students; plan ahead how best to include them in an essentially group process. Consider that there may be several reasons for their reluctance. A student may have a unique and personal story to tell and want no one else to interfere with its development. Other students shy away from group work because they are unsure of their writing skills and their ability to contribute to the scene. At this point you can accept their preference to work alone, and use whatever means necessary to get their ideas down on paper. However, you must tell them that they will have to work with the class eventually, in order to clarify what they have written.

When the Scene Is a Personal Experience

It would be great to assume that all of your students are using their imaginations to create their material. As we discussed earlier, that is not always the case. When a scene has come out of one student's personal experience, this can present serious challenges when you begin to rewrite the scene.

I always approach the rewriting and the criticism of material as though it were a piece of fiction. I took this approach several years ago after a boy had read his monologue about a drug overdose.

The monologue depicted, quite powerfully, a boy who discovered his cousin lying unconscious in the bathroom, overdosed with heroin. It revealed true emotions and sent chills down everyone's spine. The class liked the monologue, but agreed that it needed a few changes. As we began to go through it, the author became more and more withdrawn. We would change a word here, the color of a shirt there, and he would remain silent.

At one point in the discussion, a student brought up the cousin's position on the floor. In the monologue, the cousin was sprawled one way, and the student wanted him sprawled another. It was a minor point, but it was the straw that broke the camel's back. The author erupted. He shouted, "What the hell do you all know about it? You weren't there, were you? You didn't see him, did you? I was there. I saw him. You don't know shit!" With that, he ran out of the classroom.

When the class was over, I sought out the boy. On my way to his class I played over in my mind what I wanted to say to him. My thoughts ranged from, "I'm so sorry. I can't believe we were so insensitive," to, "We didn't know this was a real story. We'll change everything back to the way you had written it."

As I got to his room, I changed my mind. I was not going to apologize for what we had done, but I was going to see if he was all right. I would talk to him about his cousin, and how he was handling the tragedy. I would praise his work and tell him how powerful it was, but I was not going to apologize for trying to make it better. We may have gotten a little carried away with the criticism, but our intentions were good.

It was then I realized that whether a student's material is all fiction, all truth or a mixture of the two, it must be treated the same way: it all must be adapted to the stage and to our purposes. Much like a book is adapted for a movie, we must adapt even the truth so that it is dramatic and promotes our message.

After talking to the student for a few minutes, I realized that he was more upset about reliving the situation than with the changes we were effecting. The next day we continued to revise his monologue. It became one of our most powerful performance pieces.

The First Revision

Once the groups are satisfied that they have written what appears to be a scene or monologue, it is time for the first revision. Have each group read its material aloud to the class. Reading the material aloud is essential because, after all, your goal is to perform what is being written. Material may look great on paper, but when it is read aloud it may fall flat. This is the point where you try to transform your prose writers into playwrights.

As the scenes are read aloud, have students ask themselves one important question: Is the dialogue believable—do the lines reflect how people really talk? Too often there will be a scene in which the characters are speaking as though they jumped out of a research paper on *Ivanhoe*.

A: Excuse me, but would you please pass the salt?

The Script

B: Of course. I am very sorry. I did not know you were having difficulty reaching it.

A: That is quite all right. By the way, you look terribly depressed today, is anything wrong?

B: Yes, I am pregnant.

You get the idea—the language is stilted and totally unconvincing. Nobody will hear the message of the scene because they can't get past the language. For the same reason, you should not fill your scenes with "ain'ts," "ums," and "wadda ya thinks." At the same time, each character's language should reflect that character. Striking the right balance is another part of the learning value of the project.

If the character is a sixteen-year-old girl, she should talk like a sixteen-year-old girl. If a character is the principal of a high school, then the character should speak accordingly. One difficulty arises in a scene, for example, which depicts drunken, abusive people. Anyone who is going to punch you in the face in a fit of drunken rage will not speak politely. How graphic should the language be? Can the true-to-life words of the character actually be used? To be absolutely effective the character should be profane and abusive at the top of his or her lungs. The subsequent message would hit home, be effective and raise a few eyebrows.

Such realism, unfortunately, is not always tolerated. Even though your scenes may be using vulgarity to show how bad vulgarity is, administrators and parents are reluctant to sanction it. Be as realistic as you feel you can be in this respect. Help students make sure vulgar language is not being used in a cavalier manner and that it can be defended as necessary to promote the message of the scene. Then be prepared to rewrite the scene if reviewers decide it's not appropriate.

Revising the scenes is often a very discouraging task for both teacher and students, since there will be a good deal of criticism and much material that must be scrapped. Scenes that once seemed solid and well-organized are reduced to amorphous ideas floating around without jelling.

Have the students go back into their groups to rewrite the scenes keeping in mind all of the suggestions made in class. Assure the class that after some more work and another revision session, their work will begin to fall into place.

The Final Revision

The individual revision comes after the students have reworked the material. This time, work with each group separately; do not involve the entire class. The students should read the rewritten scenes as you give specific suggestions for revision. Explain what you think doesn't work and help fix it.

Here you must decide how much input you should have as an editor. You want the scene to be as effective as possible, but you want the material to be your students' work, not yours. Giving useful suggestions without being heavy-handed will become easier as you gain more experience.

In the final revision, the teacher must act as an objective listener. As you revise, keep in mind the goal of each scene and ask yourself if the writing achieves it.

Some questions which help define that goal may include: Are the characters vividly and truthfully presented? Is the conflict clear? Is the resolution realistic? Has any awkward language been overlooked? Is the scene dramatic? Will the scene catch the attention of the audience? Is the action too static? Does the scene contain any unintended and dangerous messages?

Ask these questions of your students and ask them to supply rewrites of the problem sections. Should the students draw a blank about a certain revision, offer your own. This process is tedious but essential. If you took all the scenes, rewrote the awkward spots and distributed them, it would be easier, but not as instructive.

When is a scene perfect? Never. You will always be fiddling with it up until, during and after performance. Follow these rewrite suggestions, don't lose your concentration and cross your fingers. It will not be until you perform the scene for an audience that you really know if it's effective. Then, ironically, it may be too late to do much about it.

Completing the scripts marks a natural break in the program. If your objectives simply encompassed writing the scenes, then you have achieved them. If you stop here, the process will have been an extremely rewarding research and writing assignment. There are a host of things you and your students can do with the completed scenes.

Perhaps there are funds available to put together a group publication that could be illustrated, bound and distributed within the class, the school or the community. The school newspaper might want to include a few pieces in an edition and solicit student and staff responses to them. Also, many schools publish a literary magazine which would be a great vehicle for certain monologues or group orals.

Become aware of writing competitions or public speaking contests and enter those materials you consider appropriate.

Most of these sensitive issues have finally come to the forefront of our educational agenda. Going public with your material will catch people's attention, further the cause of helping students in crisis and make your students proud of their hard work.

If you want to delve deeper into the program, it is time to begin the rehearsal process and set your sights on performance.

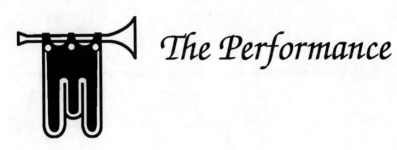

The Performance

Without a doubt, performance is the most powerful way to reach students in crisis. Something magical happens when the lights dim and a fifteen year old walks on stage to tell an audience of other fifteen year olds the story of his suicide attempt. It captures the audience's attention and, in this "MTV society," that is no easy feat.

Unfortunately, producing that magic, making it look simple, believable and unrehearsed is no easy feat either.

The following section leads you through scene selection, casting, audience and performer preparations, rehearsal and disclosure. Every step helps you to create an effective and dynamic production.

You may often want to turn back. You may be tempted to take short cuts. You may not want to deal with all of the hassles. All of these are legitimate feelings. To overcome them, remember why you began the project in the first place. Remember that by this performance, you and your students may help one young person escape an abusive situation or another think twice about suicide.

Selecting and Casting the Scenes

If you have discussed with your class the possibility that some scenes may be cut, eliminating certain scenes or people from the program will not be as difficult. But whichever way you look at it, choosing who will perform and who will not is no easy task.

This dilemma is best characterized as "performance vs. education." Do you want the absolute best performance that can be given? If so, take the handful of best actors in your class and give them all of the roles. Or do you want all of the students in your class to participate in the presentation? If that is the case, everyone will be happy but the quality of the performance may be compromised.

I was very lucky one year to have a class filled with musically talented kids. I had a piano player/composer, a drummer, and several great singers. That year we composed a few original songs and performed them during the show.

The boy who played the piano and composed the melodies for the songs worked the hardest of anyone. He wrote the original melodies, changed them to fit our lyrics, rehearsed with the singers, and generally kept the entire musical aspect of the show together. His only shortcoming was that he had a rather unappealing voice. When deciding who was to sing what song, I worked very hard to make sure that "Tom," the pianist, didn't notice that he wouldn't be singing at all. Well, he noticed.

A few days before the show (which, incidentally, was going to be performed at a conference outside of school for several hundred people) Tom came to me and asked if he could sing one verse of a certain song that had special significance to him. I didn't know what to say. The song sounded great. The girl who sang the song sounded great. Tom's piano accompaniment sounded great. Tom's voice didn't sound so great. I gave him a chance.

During a rehearsal, Tom sang the third verse of the song. It wasn't absolutely terrible, but the song was no longer great. Tom looked at me. The girl singer looked at me. The class looked at me. We all knew the truth: we knew that the quality of the song was being compromised but that Tom really wanted to sing it. I let him.

Tom and the girl performed the song at the conference. It wasn't as good as we knew it could have been, but the audience loved it. They accepted it for what it was because they were ignorant of the melodrama that preceded its debut. Most importantly, Tom was thrilled.

Tom's story illustrates that your ultimate objective is educational not theatrical. You must put your students ahead of the performance. Now, if Tom were tone deaf and insisted on singing the song, that would have been another matter. I would have had no problem pointing out to him that he couldn't sing a note. Unfortunately, most situations are not so black or white. Oftentimes, problems arise from the shades of gray. You must use judgment: your judgment as a professional, as a teacher, as a director and as a friend.

Preparing Others for the Performance
Administrators and Counseling Staff

Before you begin performing your scenes, it is essential that you have an administrator and a school psychologist view the material. As we have discussed, the perspective of an administrator or school social worker/psychologist is different than yours and is needed to find any hidden messages your material may be sending.

One year, a scene approached the subject of suicide in a humorous way. Initially, one would say that humor and suicide don't mix. After all, what's funny about suicide? But this scene used humor to make a very serious point. Tina, the main character, is writing in her diary about how empty she feels. She thinks that suicide is the only way to end her pain. All of a sudden, her fairy godmother appears. "She" was a guy dressed in long johns, a tutu, and construction boots. After he lit a cigar, his first line was, "So, you wanna kill yourself." The school psychologist wasn't pleased.

The scene progressed with the fairy godmother spewing one-liners but ultimately delivering the serious message that suicide cuts short any chance for a happy and productive future. The beauty of the scene was that we caught the audience's attention immediately with the humor, and held it until we made our point. The psychologist agreed to let us perform it and was pleasantly surprised to see how effectively it played.

The importance of having an administrator preview your scenes is obvious. You want official sanction for what you and your class have written. If a parent calls to complain about a particular scene or monologue, all you have to do is refer them to the administrator. If, however, a parent calls to praise the presentation, you can take the call yourself.

Parents

Because the program is more than a simple dramatic performance, careful planning in advance of a performance must be well thought out. One of the details that must be planned is parental contact.

If your audience is to be comprised of elementary or junior high school age children, then invite parents to a special performance either after school or during the evening. Give them an opportunity to view what their children will be seeing. Letters announcing the performance and encouraging parents to attend could be sent home via students. Invite comments, criticisms and suggestions.

Parents can provide a unique and valuable service for your program by commenting on the scenes. Ask them if they thought the parent figures were accurately depicted. Did they feel any pro-adolescent bias on the part of the student writers? Were the relationships between the young people and the adults believable?

Also, ask the parents to comment on the content of the scenes and the manner in which they were presented. Were any of them offended by explicit language? Did anyone feel that the topics were "too taboo" to confront?

Once again, it is advisable to have an administrator and/or counselor on hand to help field questions from the parents. You will be much too involved with the program to react calmly, think clearly or respond objectively.

The first time we performed for parents, it seemed as though the entire school administration had arrived. Half an hour before the performance, in the junior high auditorium sat the school's principal, his secretary, an assistant principal, the chair of the English department (who brought the principal and vice-principal of a neighboring school as her guests), a representative from the superintendent's office, and the district social worker with whom I was working.

In the audience was a couple from the community who were very active in school politics and often very critical of the administration's judgment. They were always vocal at the Board of Education meetings so there was no reason for us not to believe that they would be vocal tonight.

After the show, which focused on abortion, contraception, AIDS and teen pregnancy, we asked for comments. The administration braced themselves as the woman from the notorious couple raised her hand.

"I no longer have any children in the eighth grade, but I would still like to make one observation. This presentation was outstanding. Why didn't you do it when my children were in junior high?"

With that, we knew we were home free. In the years since that first parent performance, we have met nothing but praise, support, and positive criticism that makes our subsequent shows even stronger. Having firm parent support gives you the confidence to face their children.

Other Teachers and Student Audiences

Another important aspect of your preplanning involves the classroom teachers who will be bringing their classes to your performances. They must be prepared for what they are going to see so that they, in turn, can prepare their classes.

Preparing a class to view the production should be done the day before the students are going to see it. Ideally, no student should view the scenes cold or in a vacuum. They must be provided a context by which they can accept and interpret the information.

A week or so before the performance, meet with the teachers involved. One way to facilitate the organization of this meeting would be to call the teachers together as a department. Having your audience consist entirely of other classes in your discipline is the simplest way to perform your scripts. In this way, your organization of the meeting and your communication with the teachers will be made easy.

Consider having the support professional with whom you have been working join you at this meeting. He or she could provide valuable information regarding the severity of the issues to be handled and field any questions you do not feel qualified to answer.

I have never asked student writers and actors to attend this meeting. I feel that their presence would inhibit certain teachers from expressing problems they may have with the project or voicing any personal reservations.

You may elect, however, to have several student representatives at this meeting to provide their viewpoints on the program. Instead of inhibiting discussion, the students may serve to open some doors and some minds. In any event, the teacher and the support professional must be responsible for conducting the meeting.

At the meeting, explain the goals of the program and what you hope to achieve. Distribute a synopsis of the scenes, and review the themes and messages they contain.

Give teachers a list of target words and phrases. This list should comprise words that are the focus of the scenes, or the terms that may need to be defined before students see the performance. For example, if a scene is discussing AIDS, a definition of "HIV" may be necessary. For a date rape scene, the audience will need to understand the exact definition of the term. These definitions will help students focus their attention and will underline the seriousness of what they are about to see.

In addition to defining certain words and discussing potential themes, it is important for the teacher to actually use some of the sensitive words in class that their students will be hearing the next day.

No educator would be surprised to discover that mention of the word *sex* will get some sort of a reaction from even the most mature students. Imagine the reaction when the students are confronted with *AIDS, intercourse, rape, condoms, sexual abuse, sodomy,* etc. If these words are made public in the classroom before the show, some of the edge may be taken off of their shock value. The students will spend less time at the performance reacting to the language and more time listening to the messages.

In the past, we have found that some teachers are taken aback slightly at the mention of these terms. They do not feel comfortable discussing them and may feel unqualified in leading a discussion involving them. These are natural reactions. Teachers should be encouraged to be as specific as possible in their pre-performance discussion. However, they should not be forced into any uncomfortable situations.

Teachers who may want to avoid open discussions on sensitive issues may opt for some sort of written assignment as preparation. Students could write a conversation between two friends, one of whom is contemplating suicide. Students might research the definitions of various forms of abuse and share their findings with the class. Others could look up hotline numbers and distribute copies of a list of them.

Advise teachers to be aware of their students' reactions to the topics, scenes, themes and target words. Many students who have been abused, or who have been affected personally by one of the sensitive issues, may react negatively to the idea of a performance of this nature. Reactions may range from, "This is stupid!" to, "Why do I have to go?" These types of statements may not be indicative of any personal problems that student may be experiencing. However, such "innocent" negative reaction may indicate deeper feelings that are being suppressed.

Other possible indications to look for are students who become unusually withdrawn during the class discussion or who are absent or cutting on the day of the performance. Again, in and of themselves, these signs may be insignificant, but because of the content of the material, the teacher must be vigilant.

Some other warning signs are more blatant. Students may leave the room, begin to cry, or ask to speak to the teacher after class. Teachers must use judgment in assessing them. Is the student over-reacting? Does the student have a friend who has a problem? Is there a problem with this particular student? Each occurrence must be assessed privately and quickly to decide if the student needs to be referred to a support professional based solely upon his or her reaction to the *idea* of the presentation.

An interesting and unexpected result of teacher involvement in this section is the possibility of *teacher* disclosures.

At several pre-planning meetings I have conducted, teachers and administrators have related stories of their experiences with past abuse or with their exposure to other taboo subjects.

One administrator shared with her staff that when she was a child, she was a victim of sexual abuse. A teacher once exclaimed at a proposed scene on emotional abuse, "My god, I just said that to my seventeen year old last week!"

Whether these disclosures are serious or minor, current or years old, it is encouraging to see how far some of your colleagues will go to support your efforts. It is a good idea for the support professional with whom you are working to offer to be available should any staff member want to talk.

At your planning meeting, the teachers will ask quite a few questions and will take their role in the presentation seriously. It is essential that they fully understand the entire process because they will be on the front lines when it comes to dealing with the students before, during and after the presentations. The support and understanding of the classroom teacher is one of your most vital keys to success. You may want to share the information from the section on handling student disclosures.

There are several ways to prepare a class for the seriousness of the program. One thing is certain, the better prepared the students are, the more receptive they will be to the presentation, and the more they will learn from the experience.

Rehearsal

Plan at least three weeks for pure rehearsal and blocking. The degree of complexity with which you rehearse will vary with your drama experience and with the audience for whom you have decided to perform. If the students are to perform the scenes within the class, you need not become too fancy. If you have decided to take on the challenge to perform for an outside audience, then you have your work cut out for you.

In a classroom setting, the major difficulty of the rehearsal process is juggling the various scenes so that you may work with one group of students while the other groups work by themselves. Three weeks is not a long time to rehearse. You must depend upon the students to work diligently on their own.

I always tell the students in each scene that the more they bring to me (i.e., the more blocking, the more characterization, the more energy and commitment) the more likely their scene will make the final cut. If the students depend entirely upon you to do everything in terms of blocking and rehearsing, their scene risks not being ready for performance. It's a great motivation that simply boils down to, "The harder you work, the more likely you'll perform."

Toward the end of three weeks, have the students in the class serve both as audience and critics for scenes in which they do not perform. You may also want to invite a class of outsiders for a period to give students practice in front of an audience.

Audience Reactions

In addition to being ready with their lines, their blocking and their characterizations, the students should be ready to face their peers as actors. It is not the easiest of things to pull off.

One of the most crucial elements of the entire program concerns performing for others. Student actors will command the student audience's attention for a variety of reasons. Initially, the audience may have a certain curiosity about the actors. (Will the kids mess-up? Will they laugh? Will they make fools of themselves?) Later, the audience will be curious about the topics that are going to be covered. (Are they going to curse? Are they really going to talk about AIDS? Can they say the word "condom" on stage?)

When these questions have been addressed by the audience, you have their attention. If your material is well-written and well-rehearsed, you will keep that attention. If your work contains a fair number of weak spots, you're asking for trouble.

Discuss possible audience reactions with your student performers. Explain that even though their material is good, the audience may respond with nervousness, laughter and general "uncomfortableness." Also, the audience may be completely silent and offer no positive or negative reactions to what they are seeing.

The year we wrote and performed our own songs, we presented the show to eighth grade English classes in the bandroom of the junior high school. The location was horrendous, but because of a long list of bureaucratic complications we were forced to perform there for eight periods in a row.

I took an optimistic approach. The room was small and fostered a certain intimacy between the actors and the student audience. The audience felt they were more a part of the scene since they were, literally, two feet from the performers.

The eighth graders that year were a good audience. I was especially looking forward to a student I'll call "Grace" singing one specific song that was called "You Have the Power." The song stressed the idea that the students had control over their lives, and had the power to stop abuse and to make positive choices for themselves.

Grace had a beautiful voice and also a good deal of stage experience. The first time she sang, she moved all over the room, taking in all of the kids, singing directly into their eyes. The teachers and I were totally captivated. The eighth graders couldn't handle it. It wasn't the song or the singing that they couldn't handle; they couldn't handle a person standing two feet in front of them singing into their upturned faces. They tittered; they giggled; they whispered to each other. They never heard one word of the song.

Grace was devastated. She thought that she was at fault. After an impromptu analysis of the situation, for the next show we pulled her back, away from the audience, to put her on more of a stage. The distance we created made the song more legitimate or official. It took the pressure off the eighth graders and enabled them to be a good audience. For all of the other shows, the audience was polite and attentive.

Grace kept her composure in a difficult situation. Not all of your performers will be able to. Had we anticipated such a reaction by the audience, we would have prepared for it. But you can't anticipate everything, which is why it's necessary to tell your actors to be ready for anything.

Organizing the Performance

When you feel that everything is in place, it is time to organize your performance. As you proceed, be sure to include suggestions from your students in all of your pre-performance planning. There are quite a few things to keep in mind.

First, try to keep the audiences as small as possible. The smaller the audience, the more intimate the setting and the more likely your message will get through. Don't let an administrator talk you into doing one show for all of the sophomore English classes at one time. Even though that would make his or her job a good deal easier, it would seriously take away from the effectiveness of what you have accomplished.

You do not always have to perform in an auditorium or on a stage. Classrooms, cafeterias or gymnasiums could all be transformed into performance places. The lights, curtains and aura of a regular theatre may lend a feeling of legitimacy to your material, but they may also get in the way of your messages. The key is to know, in advance, where you will be performing and to plan accordingly. If you'll be on stage, you can use some interesting lighting effects. If you'll be in a classroom, you can scale-down the performance and make it more "real."

In addition to planning your performance space, you should carefully plot the order of your scenes and mono-logues. Pace them properly. Blend humorous scenes with serious ones. Get your audience laughing and then hit them with a heavy monologue. Intermingle your stronger scenes with your weaker ones, and, by all means, open and close the show with your two strongest scenes.

I have always tried to use musical transitions between scenes. I was lucky to have had a student drummer who worked with me for three years. He would watch the scenes the day before the show and then improvise appropriate segues. He would take into account the content of the scene and either play something fast or something mournful. Violas are great if you are looking for mournful. One violist sitting in the corner can do wonders for creating a serious tone.

If you can't muster any live music, try tapes. It is tricky to get all of the tape cues right, but the music will help keep the audience's attention during scene changes.

Try to plan to have a social worker or school psychologist introduce the presentation to the audience. After the kids are in their seats, a brief talk by a support professional sets the tone for the period. It also serves to give the audience a face with which to identify by presenting one person to whom a student might go if he or she has a problem that needs to be worked out.

Don't let the introduction go on too long. You will soon learn how long it usually takes to get an audience settled down and serious.

Performing the scenes is hard work, especially if you are going to perform them more than once in a given day.

Your actors will rise to the occasion and exhibit a sense of responsibility and maturity that you may not have seen up to that point. The material is their own and they will make sure that it is presented properly.

The performance of the scenes is also difficult for you because, essentially, your job is done. There is nothing more for you to do except watch what you helped to create. It is both a frustrating and fulfilling time, but always keep in mind that you and your students have created something that is going to help other people and you should all be very proud.

When a Performance Prompts Disclosure

When the performance is over, your job is finished; however, the process is not yet complete. One of the main objectives of the program is to foster disclosure. There must be a network in place to handle any disclosures that may come as a result of your presentation. Students who have questions, problems or friends with problems, need a pre-established place to turn.

The first person students will turn to will be the classroom teacher who took them to the show. The day following the performance, teachers should discuss with their students the themes, messages and information the scenes contained. How did the students like the scenes? Which scene was most powerful? Which was least effective? Did any student identify with one or more of the characters in the scenes?

Initially, in discussing the scenes, students may be reluctant to share their opinions. One way to open up the discussion is to ask them to remember specific moments of what they saw: Do you remember when the boy tried to kiss that girl? Do you think the blonde girl played a convincing alcoholic? Would you have smoked the joint in the bathroom?

Listen carefully to the responses to your questions. Hidden in what some students say may be a clue to a problem. For instance, a boy discussing the girl alcoholic may unknowingly reply, "She was really way off-base. My mother never acted like that." The student may not be reaching out for guidance, but implicit in the reply is the recognition of a problem.

Do not expect instant disclosures. If a student feels the need to talk, he or she probably will not blurt it out in front of thirty peers. Often, disclosures are made weeks or months after the presentation. Once again, teachers should be on the look-out for signs of kids in trouble. As we discussed earlier, be aware of students who may be uncharacteristically uncomfortable about the discussion, or for anyone who may be unusually withdrawn. Most importantly, the teacher must establish an environment that encourages and supports disclosures. A strong feeling of support and caring from a teacher may be all it takes for a student to come forward for help.

Classroom teachers should also encourage students who may want to talk, or who may have a friend who needs to talk, to seek out a support professional. If any student is uncomfortable with talking to an adult or an authority figure about an abusive situation, tell the student that confiding in a friend may be the beginning of the helping process.

Should a teacher be the person to whom a student discloses, it is essential that the teacher be aware of the fact that he or she may be legally bound to report that disclosure to school authorities. In some states, teachers and school districts have been sued because a teacher who helped a student confront an unwanted pregnancy, suicidal feelings or a drug problem failed to report the information to the administration or to the child's parents. It's a Catch-22 situation: a child can't talk to his or her parents, so he or she confides in you, and you, in turn, must immediately report your knowledge. What student would confide in a teacher knowing that the teacher is required by law to report whatever he or she is told? It is very clear that you must investigate the disclosure laws and policies of your school district and state before you even think about writing a monologue.

Another important consideration regarding disclosure concerns your student actors. Because of the work they have done, other students may view them as experts in the field and go to them with problems, questions or disclosures. The actors take on a certain credibility in the eyes of the student audience.

Sometimes, with younger audiences, we have heard remarks such as, "Look, there goes the girl who got raped," or, "Hey, that's the kid who does coke in the bathroom." Even though older audiences are more sophisticated about the student actors, they also may secretly ask themselves, "Does that kid really do coke?" or, "I wonder if her mom really is an alcoholic?" These subtle doubts or fleeting questions may imbue the student actor with an aura of trust, and audience members may turn to them for help. Should any disclosures be serious, your actors should follow the same guidelines discussed earlier in the section on handling student disclosures.

The power of theatre is strong, even when the performers are fifteen year olds in a junior high school cafeteria. If used properly, life-saving messages can be taught.

You may never see a pay-off for your weeks of hard work and dedication. You may be exhausted at the end of the process and feel that you have wasted your time because you have not heard of any disclosures made as a result of your efforts. You may swear you will never go through this process again.

Then, several weeks or months down the road, you will bump into a social worker or a guidance counselor who knows of your work. This person will tell you a story of a student in crisis and will credit you and your program for encouraging him or her to come forward.

All it takes is one disclosure to make it worth the effort, one success story to fill you with pride and to give you the energy and the courage to try again.

Sample
Scripts

T he materials in this section serve several purposes. They demonstrate the wide range of topics you may tackle and show different, creative ways to tackle them.

These scenes also provide some concrete material that may be used to augment the materials you and your students have produced.

All of these scenes, monologues and group orals were written in workshop settings by students ranging in age from fifteen to eighteen. Various teachers oversaw the process and guided the students along the way. Each scene has been performed successfully by adolescents for adolescents.

Topics range from AIDS/HIV to runaways, from emotional abuse to drug abuse. The scenes do not provide too many pat answers or happy endings. The student writers and their teachers strove to depict abusive situations realistically and to portray adolescent behavior and language authentically.

Polish these materials for performance; cite them as models; present them as discussion starters. However you elect to use them, their authors would be proud to know that their work is continuing to bridge the gap between troubled young people and the help that they desperately need.

Stage Positions

The following terms and abbreviations are used for standard stage blocking positions:

Down or Downstage (D)—the front of the stage, toward the audience

Up or Upstage (U)—the back of the stage, away from the audience

Center (C)—the middle of the stage

Stage Left (SL) and Stage Right (SR)—used in relation to the actor's left and right

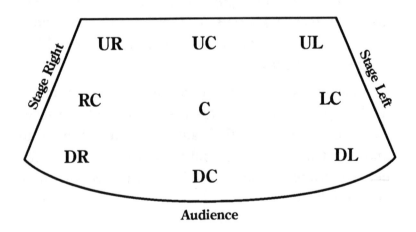

 *Abortion*

Dawn's Decision

The actor is standing DC and speaking directly to the audience.

What was I supposed to do? I don't believe in abortion, but Dawn is my best friend. Mike was completely ignoring the fact so I told her that it was her decision and no one else's. We drove there in silence: no radio, no talking, nothing...except Dawn crying. We got there, and there were all these women waiting. One girl was eleven years old. Another said not to worry because it was her fourth, and it was no big deal. They called Dawn's name and I went in with her. They took us into a dressing room and asked Dawn to put on a white robe. I wasn't supposed to go in, but Dawn was so scared she wouldn't go in without me. She wanted me there while they gave her the anesthetic. So we walked into this all white room which was shining and full of bright light. I held Dawn's hand while they gave her the needle. When she was quiet, I walked out, went into the bathroom, and threw up. I was so weak I couldn't even stand up...That was four months ago. Dawn's fine now and we both feel she made the right decision, for her. But I don't think either of us will soon forget that ride we took in silence, or the room that was shining and full of bright, bright light. (*Blackout.*)

 *AIDS/HIV*

AIDS Rap

The stage is black. On cue, a "rap rhythm" begins softly and builds in volume. The rhythm may be played on tape, on stage with a synthesizer or on drums. It is a key part of the scene and should be done well. When the music reaches its loudest point, the lights fade up to reveal a man and a woman standing with their backs to the audience. On cue, Man *turns and begins the rap.* Woman *turns on her first line. Each speaks into a hand-held mike.*

Man: Hey, you! Forget your reputation

Woman: AIDS is causing a world-wide violation

Man: And it's takin' innocent lives ya gotta see

Woman: It could take you, your mama, hey, even me

Man: But, yo, lemme' share with you a little tale that involved a school boy who attended Yale

Woman: His name was Mike
He had quite the reflexes

Man: Didn't care for nothing but for

Both: Love between the sexes

Woman: So one day he was joshing down the street

Man: A bangin' and a yangin' down on his feet

Woman: Beggin' and a pleadin' with the girl on the beat

Man: Tryin' to make her say yes—

Both: Like a dog in heat

Man: She agreed and ran to his car

Woman: Her daddy was near so she said to drive far

Man: And in a hour when they reached their destination

Woman: She gazed at him in wild expectation

Man: She kicked her heels off onto the floor

Woman: Lookin' in his eyes

Both: You know what she was there for

Man: She put her hand on his knee
He put his foot on the gas

Woman: They almost got whiplash they took off so
fast
So now the poor homeboy
It was rude

Man: Fight' hard to prove that he was no prude

Woman: Tryin' to think up an excuse

Man: To get out of this jam

Woman: Tryin' to cut her loose

Man: Without lookin' like a ham
He said, "Listen toots,
I hate to tell ya,
ain't no more condoms
so get out of my azaleas!"

Woman: She went, "Uh-uh, babes,
It ain't that easy
First ya gotta love me
And then ya gotta please me"

Man: Kinda quietly he took a cautious cough
Then he started with her again from where
he left off

Woman: But stupid him—
How was he to know
That this very fine girl

Both: Was pretty low

Woman: Catch it—

Man: She had AIDS

Woman: Got it from a needle

Man: Then passed it on to

Both: Poor Mike McDeele

Man: So now it spread to him

Woman: And there was nothin' he could do

Man: They ain't got a cure yet

Woman: As it's relatively new
And in a matter of time

Man: His friends did catch on

Woman: And he was treated as an outcast

Man: Kinda like a "non"
They kicked him around
He lived in disgrace

Woman: Suddenly he realized

Both: He was losing the race

Man: The race for time, a race of sadness

Woman: Now he's all alone
In a world gone madness
He should've used the brain that God had
gone and give him

Man: It must have been big to be bitin' Yale livin'

Woman: But instead he let his hormones do the thinkin'

Man: And they just brought him down to crashin' life sinkin'
So come on homeboys—know the situation
AIDS is causing a world-wide violation

Woman: And it's
Takin' innocent lives ya gotta see

Man: It could take you

Woman: Your mama

Both: Hey, even me ...

(Dance break which leads into the next verse.)
Woman: Pay attention—here's the thick of the plot

Man: It's about a pusher heavily into a lot

Woman: And his name was Joe

Man: Short for bastard

Woman: Drugs was the thing
         Which he had gone and mastered

Man: So one day he was hangin'

Woman: Down the corner of his block

Man: Yeah, rappin' with his buddies
         And shootin' off his mouth

Woman: He said,

Man: "Hey, yo, man
         How about a smoke?
         It's practically for nothin'"

Woman: Yeah, what a joke

Man: Ya see man
         This was one way to which he got his
         money

Woman: Givin' away free coke to the corner hangin'
         bunnies

Man: Tryin' to act like a man in order to please
his honey

Woman: And he had a drug problem

Both: And that wasn't funny

Woman: It started when the poor homeboy he was
nine

Man: Messin' with the girls and feelin' mighty
fine
Shootin' with the older boys and their crew

Man: And actin' like an animal

Both: Lock him in a zoo!

Woman: So now he was

Both: Older

Woman: Yet none the

Both: Wiser

Woman: Pushin' all those

Both: Drugs

Woman: While toastin'

Both: Budweiser

Man: Gettin' mighty

Both: High

Woman: From his excess amount of

Both: Slurpin'

Woman: Issuin' out the

Both: Gas

Man: With the belchin' and the burpin'

Woman: And then one night, his luck it all changed

Man: While boozin' with the druggies
Who were all deranged

Woman: Passin' round the goods
In the hypodermic needle

Man: While contractin' the virus
From a dude nicknamed "The Beetle"

Woman: Yeah, stupid him

Man: Was he so high

Woman: To be blinded from the fact

Man: That he was gonna die

Woman: He got AIDS

Man: Didn't want nobody to know it

Woman: Took his chances with the drugs

Both: And sure did blow it

Man: So now it was spread
There was nothin' he could do

Woman: They ain't got a cure yet

Both: As it's relatively new

Woman: And in a matter of time

Man: His friends did catch on

Woman: And he was treated as an outcast

Man: Kinda like a "non"
They kicked him around
He lived in disgrace

Woman: Suddenly he realized

Both: He was losing the race

Man: The race for time, a race of sadness

Woman: Now he's all alone
In a world gone madness

Woman: He should've used the brains that God had
gone an' give him

Man: It must've been big to be avoiding cop living

Woman: But instead he let the drugs do the thinkin'

Man: And they just brought him down to crashin'
life sinkin'
So c'mon homeboys—know the situation

Woman: AIDS is causing a world-wide violation

Man: And it's
Takin' innocent lives ya gotta see

Woman: It could take you

Man: Your mama

Both: Hey, even me

(Both dance off as the lights and the music fade.)

 *AIDS/HIV*

Facts vs. Feelings

Number One *is standing at a lectern "reading" from index cards. The delivery should be cool, factual and unemotional.* Number Two *is standing slightly DR and speaks emotionally to the audience. Number Two looks down as Number One reads, and vice versa.*

One: AIDS was first reported in 1981 as a unique syndrome characterized by a breakdown of the body's immune system. In the years since 1981, tens of thousands of men, women and children have died from the disease. Current data indicate that there is no end in sight to the suffering.

Two: I can still hear his laughter, pleading with me to remember all those great times. When we were younger, he used to read me stories.

Our favorite was "The Giving Tree" by Shel Silverstein. I used to tell him he was my giving tree because he was such a good big brother. But all that's very far away now. I take care of him because he's dying.

One: The basic facts about Acquired Immune Deficiency Syndrome are clear. A virus called HIV undermines the body's defenses against infection. The life expectancy of a person diagnosed HIV positive is tragically short.

Two: *(Crossing DR)* It doesn't matter how he got sick. It doesn't even matter that he is... *(Stops)* He's dying, and a part of me is dying with him. I come home from school and see him lying there. I cry because I love him so much. Every night I pray for him to have the strength to make it through another day. Every night I ask why this had to happen to my brother...Why does this have to happen to anyone?

One: The AIDS virus may be spread in several ways. One is through sexual contact with an infected person. Another is through sharing needles with an infected intravenous drug user. Still another way is through special contact with an infected person's blood or body fluids. Unfortunately, infected women are now giving birth to babies with AIDS. New medicines are being tested that help to postpone the development of the disease; but as of today, no cure has been found.

Two: *(Crossing to DC)* A lot of people don't understand AIDS. I really don't either. But I do understand that in a few years people won't remember how my brother used to take me bike riding, or the surprise party we threw for our parents' anniversary. All they'll remember is that he had AIDS.

One: One thing is clear, experts agree that AIDS is definitely not spread by everyday contact in a classroom or in the workplace. *(Stepping away from the lectern, relaxing the "cool" delivery, and speaking with emotion)* Facts and statistics show one side of the story. *(Walking to Number Two)* People with AIDS need all the compassion and understanding this society can give.

Two: What kind of a legacy robs a person of his pride, dignity and beauty? What kind of disease could let someone die so alone?

(Fade to black.)

 *AIDS/HIV*

People Like You

Kim *is sitting DR at one of two library tables. She has a pile of books on the table, but is looking distractedly at the floor.* Beth *is sitting slightly UL at the other table. She too has books, but she is more interested in what Kim is doing.* Steve *enters, gives Kim a kiss, and squats down next to her.*

Steve: Hey, how ya doin'?

Kim: All right ... *(Shrugs him away)*

Steve: *(Looking at all of the books)* Research? ... What's the topic? ... *(Reading)* Oh, AIDS, heavy subject. But we all know that whoever gets it deserves it.

Kim: What?

Steve: Whoever gets it deserves it.

Kim: How can you say that? Nobody deserves such a terrible disease.

Steve: OK, OK, don't be so touchy.

Kim: I mean, have you seen the faces of those poor people lying in hospital beds praying that someone will find a cure before they die? Have you read about how people are getting treated just because they have been infected and are trying to live a "normal" life? I can't believe that you actually could have said that ...

Steve: *(Cutting her off)* I was just kidding, OK? Anyway, it's not like we have to worry about that around here. Maybe if we lived in the city we would ... *(Notices that Kim is not listening)* Hey, Kim, you've been acting pretty weird for a couple of weeks now. What's up with you?

Kim: *(Snapping back)* Nothing. Really. Nothing ... Listen, Steve, I've got to get this report done by tomorrow, I'll call you when I get home. OK?

Steve: Yeah, sure ... but only if you're in a better mood. *(Kisses her perfunctorily on the cheek and leaves)*

(Lee enters the library and passes Steve as he leaves. She says hello to him, but he ignores her.)

Lee: Hi, Kim. Any idea why Steve's got such an attitude?

Kim: We just had a fight. He knows something's up with me but he doesn't know what. I should tell him, but he'll just freak out.

Lee: You tell him if and when you feel it's right. Cheer up, everything's gonna be OK.

Kim: Face it, Lee, everything is not going to be OK if you just tested HIV positive.

(Upon hearing Kim say that she was HIV positive, Beth gets up and crosses to their table.)

Beth: Well, isn't this special. Friends until the end.

Lee: Beth, what are you talking about now?

Beth: Don't play dumb with me. I just heard Kim say that she tested HIV positive. That means AIDS. Lee, if I were you, I'd keep a healthy distance.

Lee: *(Standing up and crossing threateningly to Beth)* Beth, I understand that you have a reputation for making stupid comments, but, if you don't shut up, I'm going to make you shut up.

Kim: *(Getting up and crossing to Lee)* Lee, if Beth knows, sooner or later the whole school will. They'll all think I'm a freak or something.

Beth: What else could they think? AIDS is a disease for freaks.

Lee: All kinds of people can and do get AIDS. Even *you* could get it.

Beth: I refuse to dignify that comment with a response.

Lee: Who do you think you are?

Beth: It's not me we're discussing! It's Kim here

who didn't care who she jumped into bed with!

Kim: Who cares how anybody gets sick? The important thing is, Beth, that if you think *you* are somehow immune to it, you're dead wrong.

Beth: I know what I know.

Lee: Yeah, but what you think you know is wrong.

Beth: *(To Kim)* Look, baby, it's your funeral, but don't look for any sympathy. After I get through, no one will go near you and you know it! *(Exits)*

(Steve enters, not wanting to have left Kim on such a bad note.)

Lee: *(Crossing to Steve)* Listen, Kim needs friends right now, not people to argue with.

Kim: *(Crossing to join them)* Steve, a lot of people are going to start saying a lot of things about me and most of them are not going to want me around.

Steve: Why? What do you mean? I don't understand.

Lee: It seems that not many people do. Sit down, Steve. We have a few minds to open.

(The lights fade as Lee and Kim tell Steve the story.)

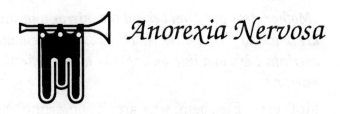 *Anorexia Nervosa*

Through the Looking Glass

Liz is standing with her back to the audience looking into a full length mirror. Both Liz and the mirror should be on a slight angle to enable as much of the audience as possible to see the reflection. Standing behind the mirror, holding it up, in view of the audience, are Rachel *(Liz's best friend)*, Liz's Mother *and a* Doctor. *Liz begins the scene by speaking to herself in the mirror.*

Liz: Look at you. *I* don't even recognize you any more. How much more weight do you want to lose? How much more weight can you lose? You may not realize it, but this is getting really out of control. You say that you don't feel right around people any more? You don't fit in? Why? You're a smart kid. *(As if listening to her subconscious)* Oh, I see, you want to get their attention. You want them to feel sorry for you. You want people to keep on saying ...

93

(Mother steps out from behind the mirror and stands with her back to the audience, off Liz's right shoulder. She overlaps Liz's last line and speaks to her reflection in the mirror.)

Mother: Elizabeth, why aren't you eating? You don't need to lose any more weight! You're skinny enough as it is. Now sit down and finish your dinner. *(Pause)* Liz, why won't you tell me what's wrong ...

(Mother crosses behind Liz and returns to behind the mirror as Rachel comes out to take her place. The movement should be circular and fluid. Rachel overlaps the last few words as she enters.)

Rachel: Tell me what's wrong! Did Chris break up with you again? Don't worry about that jerk. What reason did he give you this time? *(Listens)* Oh, give me a break! You're not the least bit fat! I didn't want to tell you, but yesterday, I saw him talking to Ellen Martin in study hall. They looked like they were getting pretty cozy!... Anyway, you're looking a little *too* thin lately if you ask me. *(Looking more closely)* Wow, and really tired, too! I hope you're not pulling that "I have to starve myself to lose weight" act again? Listen, I gotta tell you, Elizabeth ...

(Rachel crosses behind Liz as the Doctor steps out and overlaps the last word.)

Doctor: Elizabeth, your mother tells me that you haven't been eating. Is there a problem? *(Waits for an answer that is not forthcoming)* Do you feel as though you need to lose weight? *(Pause)* Has anyone else told you that you need to lose weight? *(Pause)* Well, after examining you, I say that you are perfectly proportioned. Actually, according to your height, you seem to weigh a few pounds less than you should. If anything, you need to put some weight on. I want to see you in a month, young lady! Remember no more diets ...

(Doctor crosses as Mother enters and overlaps the last word.)

Mother: Diets! All these diets! You're starting to scare me, honey. All you do is drink water and eat lowfat yogurt. You can't live like that. You're always tired but you say that you're afraid to go to sleep at night. And look at you. Your eyes are sinking into your head. Please, please, don't start to cry. I want to help. Please, let me help. You never talk...

(Mother crosses as Rachel enters and overlaps the last few words.)

Rachel: You never talk to me any more, and when you do, you wind up in tears. Have you eaten anything yet today? I haven't seen you touch food in a month and a half! You're scaring me now, Liz. I'm afraid you're going to ...

(Rachel crosses as Doctor enters and overlaps the last line.)

Doctor: I'm afraid you're going to have to take me a bit more seriously, young lady. I believe that you are suffering from Anorexia Nervosa. It is a serious eating disorder that could kill you. If this situation continues, I will be forced to put you in the hospital so that we can feed you intravenously. Do you know what that means? We will keep you on an IV around the clock to make sure that your body gets the nutrients it needs. After that, if you continue to refuse to eat, I'm afraid surgery will be necessary. We will open a section in your neck and place a feeding tube inside. You don't want that, do you? You need to eat, Miss Wilkins, or you will die. I don't want you to die ...

(Doctor crosses as Mother enters and overlaps the last line.)

Mother: I don't want you to die, Lizzie. *(Liz puts her head down.)* It's been over two months and things haven't gotten any better. *(Yelling)* Look at me when I talk to you! *(Liz looks up.)* I don't know what to say anymore! You haven't gotten your period for the past couple of months! You have no energy! Your bones are sticking out of your arms for god's sake! *(Liz looks back down.)*

(Mother crosses behind the mirror—upset and shaken.)

Mother: *(Beat. From behind the mirror, imploringly)* Look at yourself, Elizabeth.

Doctor: *(Echoing)* Look.

Rachel: Really look.

(Beat. Liz slowly brings up her head and looks at herself. Beat. Slowly, as the lights fade, she brings up her hand and touches the reflection of her face in the mirror. Blackout.)

 *Date Rape*

A Pretty Good Time

Melissa *and* Jean *are talking DR. Melissa is a quiet girl and Jean is her best friend.* Mark *and* Bob *are talking DL. Mark has the reputation as a ladies' man around school. There is a small bench both DR and DL. The girls freeze when the boys talk and vice versa. The boys are frozen as the girls begin the scene.*

Melissa: I can't believe what happened!

Jean: When?

Melissa: Last night...

Jean: Didn't you go out?

Melissa: Yeah, with Mark...he's in our philosophy class.

Jean: Whew...he's hot...

Melissa: Well, he got a little overheated last night.

Jean: What do you mean?

Melissa: He picked me up around 7:30. We were going to get something to eat and catch a movie. The food wasn't bad but I can't say that much for the restaurant. *(Freeze in conversation)*

Bob: *(Unfreezing)* So, who was the lucky girl last night?

Mark: Melissa Page.

Bob: Melissa Page? You've got to be kidding!

Mark: What's wrong with her?

Bob: Nothing! I just didn't think that she was your type...So, how was the movie?

Mark: Let's just say we never made it to the movie. *(Freeze in conversation)*

Jean: *(Unfreezing)* What movie did you guys see?

Melissa: Well...we didn't quite make it to the movie.

Jean: What do you mean you didn't quite make it to the movie? *(Freeze)*

Bob: *(Unfreezing)* So what happened? Did she dump you?

Mark: *(Smugly)* No.

Bob: You hit it off from the start?

Mark: Don't I always?

Bob: Where did you go if you didn't go to the movie?

Mark: Well, we started off at this really romantic restaurant. The food was all right but it was the atmosphere that really counted.

Bob: Mark and his magic charm won out again.

Mark: I can't take all the credit. She was quite charming herself. *(Freeze)*

Melissa: *(Unfreezing)* When we left the restaurant, the movie he wanted to see had already started. So, I suggested we go somewhere to talk and he said the beach. I've gone to the beach on other dates; I didn't think that it was a big deal. We hung out for a while and talked...

Jean: Then what happened? *(Freeze)*

Bob: *(Unfreezing)* I don't know Mark, Melissa seems kind of quiet.

Mark: That's the way they all seem until they get to know me.

Bob: Sounds like she got to know you pretty well last night!

Mark: Yeah, I guess the restaurant put her in a good mood. As a matter of fact, she got pretty friendly after dinner when we drove down to the beach. *(Freeze)*

Melissa: *(Unfreezing)* At first it was really nice. We went for a walk on the beach and talked. He even held my hand. We sat down on the sand and watched the waves...

Jean: Well...

Melissa: He kissed me. Then he kissed me again...Then, he started to get real rough. I tried to push him off, but he was too strong...

Jean: Oh my god, are you all right? Are you sure you're okay?

Melissa: I don't know—I guess so. But I'm scared. Why did this happen to me? What did I do?

Jean: You didn't do anything! Melissa, it wasn't your fault! You were raped!

Melissa: I don't know...I did go to the beach with him alone!

Jean: Yeah, maybe that was a mistake. But that does not justify what he did! What are you going to do about it?

Melissa: Do about it? What can I do? I just won't go out with him any more; or any other guy for that matter!

Jean: You could tell the police.

Melissa: Oh, sure, so everybody knows! Are you crazy? And you better not say anything to anybody either. Okay? *(Storms off)*

Jean: *(Following)* Melissa!

Bob: *(Unfreezing)* So, are you gonna take her out again?

Mark: Sure! I think she had a pretty good time last night.

(They walk off as the lights fade.)

 *Drug Abuse*

But He Wasn't Waking Up

The actor is standing DC speaking directly to the audience.

He pounded harder and harder on the bathroom door. I sat in my bedroom, staring into my math book. The banging became louder.

"Mike," he yelled. "Mike!"

My uncle forced the door open and ran in. I ran in behind him...My cousin was kneeling on the floor, leaning against the bathroom wall. A needle was lying on the floor beside him. He wasn't moving.

My uncle slapped him and shook him, but he wouldn't wake up. His arms were limp and his head hung to one side. His eyes were rolled back...

How could this happen?

Nothing like this ever happens.

I stood in the doorway just staring at my cousin...He wasn't waking up. We shook him again and screamed at him. I picked up the needle and the measuring spoon... They looked so harmless...But he wasn't waking up...

(Fade to black.)

 *Drug Abuse*

A Team Player

Carl, *the school's star running back, is DR at his locker. He is nervous because there is a big game tomorrow.* Larry *and* John *are UL with their backs to the audience. They are talking quietly.* Jim, *the quarterback, enters from SL.*

Carl: *(Tossing Jim a football as he enters)* What's up, Jim...?

Jim: Are you ready to kick some butt today? *(Slaps his hand)*

Carl: Yeah, but you better keep your arm loose! I want to see at least four touchdown passes from you tomorrow.

Jim: I'll do my best. See you at practice. *(Walks off SR)*

(Carl turns to go to class and bumps into Larry and John who have crossed to DC.)

Carl: What's up, boys?

Larry: What's up, Cool? You ready for the big game tomorrow?

Carl: I don't know, man. I'm a little nervous. I haven't had a good practice all week, and I haven't scored in three games. Plus, the coach is on my back about my grades.

John: *(Walking away, unconcerned)* That's too bad, man.

Larry: *(Pulling John DR)* John, come here for a minute.

John: What the hell are ya doing? We gotta get to lunch.

Larry: I was thinking, man, since Carl seems real down and he's pretty cool, why don't we give him some of our "blow?"

John: Why don't you go to hell! I paid a lot of money for that stuff.

Larry: Calm down. I'll give him some of mine.

John: *(Grabbing Larry's shirt)* You know I don't want a lot of people knowing about this.

Larry: Relax. Nobody's gonna find out anything. *(Turns back to Carl)* Listen, man, if you're so down, we got something to pick you up!

Carl: Yeah? What?

Larry: Coke, man.

Carl: What?

Larry: Don't act stupid. Cocaine, Slick—"blow."

Carl: What? Are you guys crazy? That shit's dangerous.

John: See, we offer it to him and he acts like a "wussie" about it.

Carl: Why don't you shut up. I just don't know if I want to do it, that's all.

Larry: There's nothing to be afraid of. Don't listen to that crap your health teacher fills you up with.

Carl: I don't know, man.

John: Hey, listen, if you change your mind, you know where to find us.

Larry: All right! We're outta here.

Carl: Later.

(John and Larry start to go off SL and Carl starts off SR. After a few steps, they all freeze. Beat. Carl then moves and establishes a boy's room. John and Larry turn and enter. The freeze denotes passage of time and a scene change.)

Carl: *(Combing his hair in the mirror)* What are you guys doing? I thought you both had class this period?

John: We do, but we needed a little break.

Larry: Now's your chance, man. We're about to cruise through the rest of the day. Go watch the door.

(Carl moves to the door as John takes out a vial of coke and a small mirror. After cutting up a few lines, Larry and John turn their backs to the audience and snort a couple. Then Larry turns to the audience and speaks to John.)

Larry: How is it, man?

John: It's ass-kickin'! *(Passes some to Carl)*

Carl: Hold up, man. I don't think I'm going to do it.

Larry: What's up, Slick! Take it!

John: Hey, if you don't want our help, then get the hell out of here and forget that you ever saw us!

Carl: You guys are messed up in the head. I thought you were my friends, but you're nothing but a couple of druggies.

John: Who are you calling druggies? *(John lunges at Carl. Larry stops him)* You just better watch your ass.

Carl: Yeah, whatever.

(Larry and John exit SL. Carl takes a few steps and freezes as before. Carl turns as Jim enters SR.)

Carl: Jim, did you get copies of the new plays Coach handed out?

Jim: Yeah, they're right here. Hey, Carl, look. *(Points over the audience)* There's a police car outside. I wonder what's going on?

Carl: I don't know, but I have a pretty good idea. Come on, let's get out of here.

(They walk off as the lights fade to black.)

 *Drug Abuse*

Trust Me

Five actors are standing in a wide semi-circle facing an empty chair. The chair is DC and is facing UC. Each actor addresses the chair as if speaking to a boy named "Johnny."

Girlfriend: Johnny, what's the matter? You forgot to call me again last night.

Teacher: John, you have been absent for the last two major exams...Is there a problem?

Mother: John, your room is a disaster and your stereo is always blaring. When are you going to develop some responsibility around this house?

Pusher: *(Breaking out of the semi-circle and moving L to R as he speaks to the empty chair)* John, I understand what's happening to you, man, and I got something that can help...Here, try this...trust me...we've been friends since second grade, remember?

(On the word "remember," all characters except the Pusher move to another location in the semi-circle. Music or drums may accompany this change.)

Girlfriend: *(Beginning as soon as all actors have changed positions)* Johnny, we had a date last night! I sat waiting for you for over an hour. Where were you?

Teacher: Your attendance has been miserable, and it is beginning to be reflected in your grades. You're a bright boy. You can do better than this.

Mother: Where were you last night? I sat up until 2:30 waiting for you to get home. You are grounded until we can get some things straightened out.

Pusher: *(Crossing R to UC as he speaks)* John, I really want to help you out, but you gotta help me out too. I know it's expensive, but we all gotta make a livin'...lighten up...

(All characters except Pusher move to another location.)

Girlfriend: *(Beginning as soon as all actors have changed positions)* John, maybe if you would talk to me once in a while we could work this out. But we never even see each other anymore. I thought it was just me, but everyone is noticing a difference in you. Maybe we should just stop going out at all.

Teacher: I've tried to help you, John, but I can do only so much. You have to meet me halfway. You failed the marking period, but let's try to get you to pass for the year...What do you say?

Mother: Johnny, you had better straighten up. You're becoming lazier and more rude every day...and, you're hardly ever home. When you are home, you're always asleep! We didn't raise you to behave this way...I also want you to stop hanging around with those new friends of yours. They're no good. Your father is ready to throw you out. Is that what you want?

Pusher: *(Crossing from UC to DR as he speaks)* Don't listen to them, Johnny, listen to me. If I listened to all those fools I wouldn't be where I am today. You're doin' fine. You gotta look out for yourself first! Trust me... Trust me... *(Actors change positions.)*

(As the Girlfriend is speaking, the Pusher is crossing to just off her right shoulder.)

Girlfriend: I want to help you Johnny, but you won't let me...

Pusher: What does she know? You know what's important. You don't need her. You just need this. *(Holds out his hand to the chair)*

(As the Teacher is speaking, the Pusher is crossing to just off his right shoulder.)

Teacher: You're on your last legs, John. Turn it around. Turn it around, now! This may be the last chance you get.

Pusher: School is just a waste of time. Teachers don't care. They just want to cause trouble for us. Don't listen to him.

(As the Mother is speaking, the Pusher is crossing to just off her right shoulder.)

Mother: You're not going to survive this, son. Stop, please.

Pusher: Your mother was gonna throw you out of the house. Why should she care what you do now? She doesn't care anything about you!

Girlfriend: *(Throws down a varsity jacket)* That's it! It's over! *(Turns her back on the chair)*

Teacher: Is this what you wanted? Is this what you really wanted? *(Turns his back on the chair)*

Mother: That's it! I've done all I can do! Now you are on your own! *(Turns her back on the chair)*

(After the Mother turns, the Pusher looks around at all of the people who have, literally, turned their backs. The Pusher then walks slowly over to the chair, puts his right foot up on it, looks directly at the audience and smiles wickedly as the lights fade to black.)

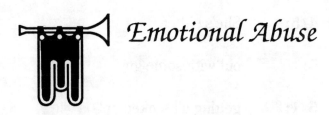 *Emotional Abuse*

It's Been a Real Long Time

Five actors are standing in a tableau. Their lines should effectively overlap to give the impression that only one actor is indeed speaking.

1:   It's been a real long time since I've seen my mother...

1/2:   I mean, yeah,

2:   sure, I see her before I go to bed

2/3:   and she's there when

3:   I wake up, but those are the only times I

3/4:   see

4:   my mom. Mostly,

4/5:   She's either

5:   out with some guy

5/1:   getting all "coked-up"

1:   or getting so drunk

1/2:   that she'd come home

2:   and throw the keys across the room;

2/3:   always hitting something new.

3:   The worse thing about it is that she'd never

3/4:   remember

4:   what happened the day before.

4/5:   I'd be sleeping and

5:   she'd storm in and start hitting me.

5/1:   Not one of those slaps

1:   you get for making a wise-assed comment.

1/2:   It's the kind

2:   you get across the face with a leather strap

2/3:   when you don't get the milk home on time.

4:   Sometimes she would just throw all my books at me and say:

3:   "Get the hell out of the house and don't screw up in school!

1/2/5:   And don't bother coming home

1:   'cause if you do

1/2:   you will regret

1/2/3:   ever being

All: born!"

3:   The next morning she'd be sober

4:   and things would be back to normal.

5:   Normal!

1:   Whatever that is.

2:   Yeah.

4:   Yeah.

3:   Yeah.

5:   Yeah.

1:   It's been a real long time since I've seen my mother.

(Blackout.)

Runaways

I'm Sorry

Four actors are standing in a tableau, speaking directly to the audience.

1:   Hello?

All: Is anyone home?

1:   I guess not.

2:   Then again, why should today be any different. Mom

3:   and Dad are

3/4:   never here

4:   when I get home from school. I guess Mom's out working her second job. I really

3/4: feel sorry for her.

3: She works so hard. I don't even want to know where Dad is.

All: Dad.

3: I don't know why I call him Dad.

1: He's the one person I don't feel sorry for.

4: What does he do? He

4/2: sleeps all

2: afternoon. Then,

4: he gets up,

3: goes out to some sleazy bar,

1: and stays there for hours until he is so drunk he can hardly walk home.

2: When he does get home, he

2/3:   goes back

3:   to sleep until the next day.

3/4:   Another afternoon

4:   when he wakes up and doesn't know what day it is.

1:   A lot of times he comes in about

1/3:   four in the morning.

3:   Mom actually sits up

3/2:   all night

2:   and waits for him. I wonder, how can she really care whether he

2/1:   comes home or not?

1:   I asked her the other night why she

1/4:   stays with him.

4:   She said...

All: "He's my husband and I love him."

4:   How could she love him after

4/3:   all the things

3:   he does to her? He lies to her.

2:   He yells at her.

4:   He steals money from her.

1:   He even hit her once. She said...

All: "Oh, it was just one time."

3:   "He was just a little drunk."

2:   "He told me it would never happen again."

1:   And she believed him!

3:   If she only knew...

1:   I wish so much that

1/4:   I could just

4:   scream at her and say

3:   "Would you

All: wake up!"

3:   It's not going to stop.

2:   It will just get worse.

4:   It will just go on

2:   and on

1:   and on

3:   and on until he really hurts you!

2:   Believe me, he's said it to me, too. Every time he

3/4:   Sobers up

4:   he says, "I'm sorry..."

1:   I'm sorry.

3:   "It won't happen again..."

1:   I'm sorry.

4:   "You're my little kid and I love you..."

1:   I'm sorry.

4:   And I love you.

2:   Love.

1:   His little kid, yeah, right!

1/3:   He doesn't have a little kid when he's drunk.

4/2:   He has nobody but himself.

4:   So, I'm running away. I know it's wrong, but what other choice do I have?

3:   *(After 4 says "I'm running away"—like a round)*

So, I'm running away. I know it's wrong, but what other choice do I have?

2: *(After 3 says "I'm running away")* So, I'm running away. I know it's wrong, but what other choice do I have?

1: *(After 2 says "I'm running away")* So, I'm running away. I know it's wrong, but what other choice do I have?

All: What other choice do I have?

(Blackout.)

 *Safer Sex*

When Elvis Was King

All actors are frozen on stage in positions that denote their characters. They are in an improvised drug store. The Narrator is frozen UC and begins the scene by walking DC. As she speaks, the other characters remain frozen until they are introduced to the audience.)

Narrator: *(Speaking as she walks DC)* In the fifties, when Elvis was king, sex was a very hushed-up subject. But is it any wonder? I mean, even if you wanted to be smart about sex, buying contraceptives was no easy task. Witness the following situation, circa 1958. Our scene opens in a local drug store with an obnoxious salesperson *(Sue moves into position with her clipboard; taking inventory.)*, a lazy stockboy *(Scott moves into position and begins to sweep the floor.)*, and a very nervous customer. *(Dan enters the store.)*

Dan: *(Nervous, fidgeting)* Excuse me...

Scott: Hey, Danny! How are ya? Whada ya doin' in this dump?

Dan: Uh, how are ya doin'? I'm looking for, um... *(Cough)*... cough medicine. Yeah, that's it *(Cough)* cough medicine.

Scott: Last time I looked it was over in aisle four.

Dan: Thanks. Thanks a lot.

Scott: No problem.

Sue: *(Looking up from her clipboard)* Scott, get back to work. I'm not paying you to socialize.

Scott: Yeah, yeah, I'm goin'. I'm goin'. *(Moves off sweeping reluctantly)*

Sue: *(Noticing Dan nervously looking up and down the aisles)* Is there something I can help you with?

Dan: Well, now that you mention it, I need...um.. well, ya see I...um...

Sue: What? I ain't got all day.

Dan: Well, ya see, I got this big date tonight with Ida Louise MacIntyre and I...

Sue: I'm not interested in your personal life. *(Starts to leave)*

Dan: Wait! I need... *(Whispers in her ear)*

Sue: What? That's disgusting! Does your mother know you're here?

(Dan runs out and all characters resume their original frozen positions. As they move, the characters should change some minor piece of costume to indicate that it is now present day. When all characters are in position, Narrator resumes by walking DC.)

Narrator: Today, things have changed. With the spread of AIDS and sexually transmitted diseases, "condom" is no longer a dirty word. In fact, everyone from the surgeon general to the general public stresses their importance. Witness our next scene. It's the same local drug store with a different salesperson and the same lazy stockboy, thirty years older. As you'll see, things are a bit different.

Scott: *(Obviously thirty years older, still sweeping and now singing)* When I get older, losing my hair, many years...

Dan: *(Entering with his arm around* Ida Louise*)* Scotty, how's it goin'?

Scott: Ah, okay I guess, but after thirty years in this dump it gets harder and harder to keep sweeping and cleaning and... *(Moving off stage sweeping and mumbling)*

Sue: *(Calling)* Scott, get back to work, I'm not paying you to socialize.

Scott: I'm goin'...I'm goin'.

Dan: Later, Scotty...

Ida: Take care of yourself, Scott.

Dan: *(Moving to Sue)* Excuse me, do you sell contraceptives?

Sue: Yeah, sure, down aisle four. Right over there.

Dan: Thanks.

Sue: Is that it?

Dan: Yes, thanks.

Ida: *(Pulling Dan aside)* Danny, are you sure we're doing the right thing?

Dan: Listen, whatever we decide to do or not to do later isn't it best to play it safe?

Ida: *(Smiling)* It sure is.

(Dan and Ida freeze. Narrator moves DC and stands between them.)

Narrator: *(To the audience)* As you have seen, attitudes towards sex and sexuality have become much more open over the years.

Ida: *(To the audience)* Contraceptives of every kind can be purchased right off the shelves.

Dan: *(To the audience)* The AIDS epidemic and the

rise of other sexually transmitted diseases have put emphasis on personal safety.

Sue: The message now is: protect your health—protect your life.

Scott: Abstinence before marriage is one answer and personal protection is another.

All: Remember—ignorance kills.

(Blackout.)

 *Sex Education*

The Guest Speaker

The stage is empty except for a lectern. Students 1-7 are sitting with the audience pretending they are there to watch the scene. Dr. Margaret Griffen *walks on stage and takes her place behind the lectern. She should look as scholarly as possible; even a touch pompous.*

Dr. Griffen: Good morning my fellow teachers. My name is Dr. Margaret Griffen. I'm from the state advisory committee on teenage sexuality. I have been asked to speak with you today about the new approach the state is taking with our sexual education curriculum...To begin, we have redefined our terms. We are no longer referring to this curriculum as "sex education." We believe that this term carries too much "negative baggage," if you will. Therefore, for the remainder of my talk, I will refer to "sex education" as "Student Interpersonal Nature." We believe that educators must stress the interpersonal nature of sexual activity rather than the purely physical aspects.

Student 1: *(Raising hand but remaining seated)* Excuse me, Dr. Griffen...

Dr. Griffen: Yes?

Student 1: Does your curriculum include a discussion of sexual abuse?

Dr. Griffen: Of course. But the way we differ from our old approach to that subject is that we avoid any graphic definition of the abusive act. We focus instead on the interpersonal nature of the abuse. We feel that...

Student 2: *(Standing)* Dr. Griffen, how do you address teen pregnancy in your curriculum? *(Sits)*

Dr. Griffen: We believe that the less said on that subject the better. We don't want to fuel any fires with heated classroom discussion. Teenagers generally ignore...

Student 3: *(Speaking a bit more loudly from seat)* What about contraception?

Dr. Griffen: Contraception is briefly touched upon in

the later chapters. But let me stress once again that...

Student 4: *(Speaking more loudly)* Do you ever use the word "condom?"

Dr. Griffen: *(Getting flustered)* Condom?...

Student 5: *(Standing and speaking still more loudly but without rudeness)* Yeah, and what about AIDS?

Student 6: *(Shouting from seat)* And abstinence?

Dr. Griffen: Wait a minute here! Where is the principal? *(Addressing an imaginary principal at the back of the house)* I was told that this audience would be made up entirely of adult professionals. These people are clearly students. I don't feel that they should be part of our discussion. They should not be involved!

Student 7: *(Calmly but firmly from seat)* We're already involved.

Dr. Griffen: What was that?

Student 7: *(Standing)* You're too late, Dr. Griffen. Most teenagers are already involved in sex and sexuality in one way or another.

Dr. Griffen: I'm sure that I don't understand your point.

Student 7: Your committees and your speeches do nothing but skirt the very issues every student needs to confront.

Dr. Griffen: I beg to differ. We're educators. We're professionals. We're adults!

Student 7: We're the ones getting pregnant! Why don't you ask us what we think about sex education before you begin writing all of your special programs?

Dr. Griffen: Do you think that you could do a better job?

Student 7: I think that we can help do a better job!

Dr. Griffen: *(Pausing to consider and then relaxing her hostile tone)* Young lady, we must talk!

(Dr. Griffen walks into the audience and leaves engaged in a serious conversation with Student 7 .)

 *Sex Education*

Sexually Speaking

A small woman, who may have a thick German accent, is sitting at the center of a semi-circle of chairs. She is the hostess of a talk show called "Sexually Speaking." She begins the scene by looking into the audience as though she were speaking into a camera.

Doctor: Hello! This is the Doctor and we are sexually speaking! Today we will be discussing the different views on sex education in the public school. Let's take our first caller. *(Pushing an imaginary phone button)* Hello, you are on the air with the Doctor.

Vinny: *(From off stage)* Yeah, Doc, this is Vinny Bartolucci from Brooklyn, New York and I watch your show all the time.

Doctor: Why thank you, Vinny. Now, why have you called?

Vinny: Uhh, I, uhh, sorta have this problem.

Doctor: And what problem is that?

Vinny: It's my girlfriend.

Doctor: Oh, yes. Doesn't she want to—ah—you know?

Vinny: No, that's not it.

Doctor: Are you putting too much pressure on her, Vinny?

Vinny: No, no, that's not it either.

Doctor: Well, then, what's the problem? Do want to, ah, "you know?"

Vinny: I feel, I feel that she's rushing things a little.

Doctor: *(Slightly embarrassed)* Oh, I see. Well, how do you feel about that?

Vinny: I don't think I'm ready.

Doctor: Vinny, listen to me. Never be rushed by anyone or anything. Do you hear me? You make the decision. When and if you do feel comfortable remember, take the necessary precautions and use contraceptives. Okay?

Vinny: Yes, Doctor, I will. Thank you.

Doctor: Promise, Vinny?

Vinny: Promise.

Doctor: Good...My first guest in the studio is a seventeen-year-old young man from Little Loop, Louisiana. Please welcome, Mr. Eugene Finkelstein.

Eugene: *(Walking in from SR and sitting next to the Doctor. Eugene is an awkward boy and is very nervous to be on television.)* Hello, Doctor. I'm really glad to meet you. Thank you for inviting me on your show.

Doctor: You're welcome, Eugene. Now, could you please tell me your views on sex education in the public school setting?

Eugene: Well, I don't see anything wrong with it. Teen-agers of today should be educated in all areas of life and sex is certainly one real big part of life, wouldn't you say?

Doctor: I most certainly would.

Eugene: My parents didn't believe in sex education so they let me fend for myself and look how I turned out... *(Snorts)*

Doctor: Good point there. It looks to me, Eugene, that you are a bit shy around the young ladies, am I right?

Eugene: Well, no, not really.

Doctor: Eugene, have you ever taken a young lady on a date?

Eugene: I once took Beatrice McKinney to a Star Trek Convention in Baton Rouge. Is that a date?

Doctor: Sure it is. Did you have a nice time?

Eugene: I think so. But...

Doctor: But what, Eugene? What is the problem?

Eugene: We didn't do anything.

Doctor: That's not a problem.

Eugene: But don't all normal teenagers have sex?

Doctor: No, no, no, Eugene. Everyone is different. Take your time...follow your own time clock, so to speak. You'll know when the time is right. Oh, and remember, be smart, use contraceptives.

Eugene: Thank you, Doctor.

Doctor: Thank you. Let's take another caller *(Pushes another imaginary phone button)* Hello, you are on the air with the Doctor.

Grace: *(From offstage)* Hi, Doctor, this is Grace from East Riverdale, Rhode Island.

Doctor: Yes, Grace, go right ahead.

Grace: Can you get pregnant from heavy petting?

Doctor: Excuse me?

Grace: My mother always told me that you can get pregnant from intense kissing on the first date or any time after that.

Doctor: Excuse me, Grace, but would you mind telling me your age?

Grace: Twenty-seven.

Doctor: And no one has ever explained to you about sex?

Grace: Well, my parents were too nervous about the whole thing, and we didn't have sex education classes in school, so, I guess not.

Doctor: Grace, to answer your question, no, you cannot get pregnant from heavy petting...and dear...promise me you'll call your mother and talk, okay?

Grace: Okay, thanks.

Doctor: Thank you for calling. Bye. My next guest is

a sixteen-year-old young man. Please welcome Mr. Ramone.

Ramone: *(Walking in very confidently)* Hey, wassup
Doc? *(Slapping Eugene on the back)* Hey,
Eugene...*(Sits on the other side of the Doctor)*

Doctor: *(Cough)* Mr. Ramone...

Ramone: Just Ramone.

Doctor: Okay, Ramone, what school do you attend?

Ramone: High school, yeah that's it, high school.

Doctor: Very good, Ramone, but, ah, let's get to our
subject here...Do you have a girlfriend?

Ramone: I got lotsa girlfriends.

Doctor: That's nice, Ramone, but tell me, how do you
feel about sex education in public schools?

Ramone: I don't need no sex education in school.

Doctor: No? And why is that?

Ramone: I can watch my movies at home.

Doctor: Well, what about other teenagers in school?

Ramone: Aww, let 'em get their own movies...

Doctor: Uh, no, what I mean is, should they be taught sex education in school?

Ramone: Yeah, sure.

Doctor: And what is your reasoning behind this?

Ramone: Well, you see, since we realize the complexity of the AIDS epidemic and with the resurgence of STDs, sex education in school is more essential than ever. It is a vital element of the school curriculum.

(Eugene and the Doctor look at one another in amazement.)

Doctor: My goodness, Mr. Ramone, how surprisingly enlightened of you.

Ramone: Just Ramone!

Doctor: Thank you very much, Ramone...My next guest in the studio is an experienced elementary school teacher from Appletown, Iowa. Please welcome, Mrs. Ethel Lillian Wipple.

(Ramone stands and offers Ethel his chair. After she sits in it, Ramone forces Eugene out of his and sits down. Eugene then goes and sits next to Ethel.)

Ethel: *(To Ramone)* Why, thank you, young man...I think...Is that the camera? Oh, hi boys and girls. I would like to say hi to all of my young friends back home...Hi Johnny, Mary, Sue, Greg, Danny, Susie, Scott. Hello to Missy, Michelle and...

Doctor: Mrs. Whipple, please...Thank you. Now, tell me, do you feel sex education should be taught in public school?

Ethel: Well, now come to think of it, I think that sex education should be taught as soon as possible. I know I would want my fourth graders to learn about the birds and the bees.

Doctor: You don't see a problem with talking to fourth graders about sex?

Ethel: Not if it's done in a sensitive way and the subject is presented so they can understand it at their young age.

Doctor: From your experience, do you think that the kids of today know a lot about sex?

Ethel: I think that a great many of the kids of today are misinformed about sex. They hear things from their friends and from other people and they get the wrong messages. We have to remember that one day, all of my cute, little, darling fourth graders *(Waves to the camera)* will, one day, grow into foul-mouthed, obnoxious teenagers. *(Gives Ramone a dirty look)*

Ramone: *(With an attitude)* Are you talkin' to me?

(Ramone and Ethel begin an ad lib argument as the Doctor begins to speak.)

Doctor: Well, that's all for today's show...Have a nice day, and, oh, remember, be smart, use contraceptives...

(Ethel and Ramone continue to argue as the lights fade to black.)

 *Sexual Abuse*

The First Time

The actress is sitting against the side wall of the stage with her knees tucked under her chin. She is gently rocking as she speaks.

He came into my room again last night. This time he sat at the edge of my bed and stroked my hair. I just stayed quiet; knowing he could feel me wince when he touched me.

I was so scared. I tried to block him from my mind. What did I do that was so wrong? What have I done to deserve this? I would start to think about the summer and the beach and my friends...then I would feel his hand touching my face again. I was lucky. He was tired. He had worked all day. Usually he's not satisfied with so little.

I remember the first time. He had come into my room as he did last night, only it was different. It wasn't enough for him just to sit at the edge of the bed...something about it being cold. No matter how hard I pushed him away, it was no use...he forced me.

When he was finished, he left. He went out. I don't know where. I remember crying and crying all curled up under the covers praying to God to forgive me for the awful thing that I had done. I rocked back and forth 'til I fell asleep.

The next night, I decided I wasn't going to let it happen again. I was going to be tough. I put up a fight; kicking, screaming, the whole bit. What a mistake...He beat me bad that night, so bad that I couldn't move. But it didn't matter to him. He did what he came to do.

After he left, I went into the bathroom and threw up until I had no strength left. I just stayed on the floor in a heap until I heard him come home. Then I got into the shower and I scrubbed my skin raw; hoping to get rid of the dirtiness I felt.

I hate him. I hate my father.   *(Blackout.)*

 *Sexual Abuse*

The Promise

Cindy and Dawn are sitting in Cindy's living room studying for tomorrow's final in biology. Cindy's Father enters, having come home from work.)

Father: *(Off stage)* Cindy...Cindy, I'm home. *(Entering)* Oh, who's your friend?

Cindy: Dad, I'd like you to meet Dawn... *(Ad lib greetings)*

Father: Cindy, did you start dinner yet?

Cindy: No, Dad, not yet...

Father: Did you run the vacuum this morning before you went to school?

Cindy: No, sorry.

Father: Well, did you at least do the laundry?

Cindy: I started to, but Dawn and I were studying for the bio final tomorrow and...

Father: I see. Finish up here with your friend and get started with my dinner. *(Exits)*

Cindy: *(Picking up the books)* Things are busy around here. My father is a...

Dawn: I understand, really. I've gotta get going anyway. Just make sure you...

Father: *(Storming in and confronting Cindy)* Did you say that you started the laundry? *(Catching her arm and turning her toward him)* Answer me!

Cindy: Here we go again.

Father: What was that?

Cindy: Nothing.

Father: Every time I come home from work you are

always goofing-off with one of your friends and doing whatever the hell you please!

Dawn: Listen, I better be getting home. I'll call ya later, Cindy. Nice meeting you, Mr. Sommers.

Cindy: Don't forget to call, Dawn.

Dawn: I won't. Bye. *(Exits.)*

Father: If your mother were around you wouldn't be acting like this.

Cindy: If my mother were around, a lot of things would be different.

Father: Like what?

Cindy: Like...

Father: Well?

Cindy: *(Walks away from her father, stops and then turns to confront him.)* Like the way you treat me. You are always yelling, and making me do all the work around the house.

Father: You know full well that since your mother's death I just can't do...

Cindy: ...and like the way you touch me.

Father: What?

Cindy: You make me feel dirty. I don't care what you say, it's wrong!

Father: *(Getting caught off guard)* Don't you talk to me like that! I'm your father and you do as I tell you!

Cindy: *(Crying)* But, Daddy...

Father: *(Coming over to her)* Honey, *(Putting his arm around her)* you know that I love you and would never do anything to hurt you... *(Getting closer)* Don't you love your...

Dawn: *(Walking in quickly)* I'm sorry, I forgot my... *(Startled, the Father leaves quickly. Dawn turns to Cindy.)* Are you all right?

Cindy: Don't worry. It's really no big deal. This happens all the time.

Dawn: No big deal? You don't have to put up with this kind of abuse.

Cindy: It's not abuse. He's my father...I better go start his dinner.

Dawn: *(Stopping Cindy)* Cindy, wait.

Cindy: Forget it, Dawn! Just forget it. Please. You'll make things worse than they are. If you want to help me, you won't say anything to anyone about this! Ok?...Promise?...Dawn?

Dawn: *(Confused and not knowing what to say)* Cindy, I...

Cindy: Promise me!

Dawn: Cindy, I can't.

(Cindy exits quickly, and Dawn stands on stage alone as the lights fade to black.)

 *Suicide*

Jennifer

A man or woman standing alone, visibly upset.

Jennifer was beautiful, intelligent and always fun to be with. I thought we had the perfect friendship. We shared everything, and we were always open and caring.

Jennifer's mother died three months ago and she was crushed. I mean she was totally depressed. She walked around with this empty stare all the time. She became moody. She was happy one second and crying the next. All of her friends were worried about her. Jennifer told everyone, even me, to just leave her alone 'cause she'd be all right.

Last month I began to notice other changes in her. She just didn't care how she looked. Her clothes were wrinkled, her hair wasn't combed and she wasn't wearing any make-up. Jennifer was always tired and was falling asleep in her classes. Her average dropped from an "A" to a "D" and she didn't care.

Jennifer wasn't eating, either.

This last week had been the hardest since her mom died. First, she found out she was two months pregnant. She knew the only person she'd ever been with was Mike, a high school drop-out. It had happened the night she got drunk trying to forget her mother's death. Jennifer knew she couldn't bring herself to have an abortion, and the thought of having a baby scared her to death. Then came the family emergency. Her father had to go to California to help her aunt who was in the hospital with cancer.

I guess Jennifer felt alone. I tried to call her all week but I didn't get an answer. I was really worried about her and went over to her house two or three times but that didn't help either.

I thought she knew I was always here; always willing to help. I guess I was wrong.

Yesterday, Jennifer's father came home. He found Jennifer hanging in the bathroom. She had committed suicide. She left a real short note.

Once there was a girl named Jennifer. She was beautiful, intelligent and fun to be with. She was my friend and I will miss her.

(Fade to black.)

 *Suicide*

Tina and the Fairy Godmother

Tina *is sitting on a small bench that is DC and positioned about two feet in front of another identical bench. Both benches are in front of a closed, black curtain. Tina is writing in her diary as she speaks.*

Tina: Dear diary, I'm really scared. Nothing is going right. My life is so...empty. I just can't shake this bad feeling. I should just lie down and die. That would solve everything.

(As Tina continues to write, the curtain behind her begins to move. Someone is obviously trying to get through it with little success. Grumbling noises are heard. Finally, the curtains separate and out pops Tina's Fairy Godmother. Tina is oblivious to the character making his way to the bench behind her. He is wearing a tutu, long johns and a blonde wig, and is chewing on an unlit cigar. He steps up on the bench and begins to speak.)

Fairy: Oh no, not another one. *(Tina falls off the bench and the Fairy Godmother lights his cigar.)* So, you wanna die?

Tina: No, I...I don't want to die, but it's the only way I know to stop the pain.

Fairy: It'll do more than just stop the pain. Honey, let me tell you something. I've been dead for goin' on 249 years now, and I'll tell you a little secret: it's not all it's cracked up to be. Pain? Talk about pain! I've had the worst rheumatism for the better half of the last century.

Tina: But you don't understand! I'm not wanted. My friends don't invite me anywhere, and my parents have no time for me. No one notices me...this will make them notice!

Fairy: Yeah, they'll notice. *(Walks over to an imaginary coffin and looks down at an imaginary body)* "Oh, my, what a pretty dress they've laid her out in." *(Changing voices and characters)* "She looks so natural!" *(Changing characters again)* "I hear she slit her wrists in a bath tub! Tsk, tsk!"

Tina: Stop! Stop! I get the picture! But tell me, what do I have to look forward to? Two more years of high school, the same people every day, no friends, no future?

Fairy: Pushing-up daisies for the rest of eternity is a future I'd be happy with. Hey, I didn't want to do this but...Tina, this can be you in fifteen years!

(Through the black curtains walks Tina-of-the-Future. She is dressed in a business suit and is dictating briskly to a male secretary who walks three steps behind her. She moves DR and mimes dictation.)

Fairy: Meet Tina Myers, Vice-President of the Powers Corporation.

Tina: *(Incredulously)* That's me?

Fairy: And this is your husband...

(Through the black curtains now walks a distinguished-looking man. He walks up to Tina-of-the-Future and puts his arm around her. They then freeze in a blissful tableau.)

Tina: *(Walking over to the frozen threesome)* All right! This is incredible! I'm gonna be rich.

I'm gonna be married to a millionaire. I'm gonna be happy!

Fairy: *(Beat)* You ain't gonna be here!

(Tina-of-the-Future, her husband, and her secretary walk off the stage briskly. Tina is left staring at an empty stage.)

Tina: What?

Fairy: You're gonna be dead!

Tina: Are you telling me that if I don't kill myself I will have all that?

Fairy: What do I look like, your fairy godmother?

Tina: I meant to ask you about that outfit you have on.

Fairy: Listen, I guarantee you that if you kill yourself, you won't have a chance to have any of that. At least now, while you're still breathing, the odds are in your favor.

Tina: I see your point.

Fairy: Good. Now remember, even though there may be a few bumps along the way, the future is worth waiting for. *(Looks at his watch)* Wow, gotta fly. I'm doing lunch with Elvis in twenty minutes. *(Exits)*

Tina: *(Returning to her diary)* Dear diary, we've gotta figure some things out.

(Lights fade.)

About the Author

R. William Pike, MA, is a writer, educator and director who has worked for over fifteen years to employ theater as an educational tool. He has taught high school since 1978; helped to develop a language arts textbook series; directed plays for several regional theaters; and has written on the arts for various publications and lectured on the subject of using theater in the classroom. Mr. Pike is currently developing a workshop which teaches both young people and adults how to use theater effectively to help young people in crisis.